ARTHUR CALEY
THE MANX GIANT

JOHN QUIRK

THE AMAZING STORY OF
ARTHUR CALEY
THE MANX GIANT

JOHN QUIRK

Manx Heritage Foundation

Published by the Manx Heritage Foundation,
P O Box 1986, Douglas, Isle of Man IM99 1SR.
www.manxheritage.org

Copyright John Quirk &
Manx Heritage Foundation 2009

First published 2009

ISBN 978-0-9562064-4-2

British Library Cataloguing in Publication Data
A catalogue record for this book is available from the British Library

Layout and typesetting by
The Manx Heritage Foundation

Printed and bound in Wales by Gomer Press Limited, Ceredigion

Dedication
To Dad—two feet (give or take) shorter than Caley, but still a giant.

CONTENTS

ILLUSTRATIONS

The publishers would like to acknowledge the kind permissions from the Miller Family for use of the illustration on page 42, the Bibliothèque Nationale de France for the illustration on page 33 and to ACRPP for the illustration on page 35. Also to the Manx National Heritage Library for the illustrations on pages 16, 18, 21, 37, 39, 44 and 78.

ACKNOWLEDGEMENTS

With any book that sees the light of day, the author is always indebted to a long list of people who offered help, advice and support, and this project has been no different:

To Carlton, for his understanding and unstinting support as I pulled together the various strands of research; Charles Guard of the Manx Heritage Foundation for his infinite patience and skill in designing the book you now hold and Ruth Sutherland for the superb cover design; Sabine Moreno for her thorough research in Paris; Billy Graham, for indulging me in tales of yesteryear on a visit to the cottage at The Well; John Hall and Alex Mealin for their superb photography; Kirsty Neate, Curatorial Services Officer at Manx National Heritage; the staff at New York Public Library's online 'Ask' service; Alessandra Wood, Curatorial Assistant at the Barnum Museum, Bridgeport; Erin Foley, curator at the Baraboo Circus Museum Research Center, Wisconsin; Frances Coakley; Terence Brack and his family; John and Joan Callow of Rose Cottage; Julian and Vivien Teare; Duncan Cochrane and Rowan Ross, and Andrew Ravenscroft. If I have missed anyone's name from this list, my sincere apologies to you.

Finally, as always, my love and thanks to Emma, Ryan and Gypsy-Mae, for putting up with me. Again.

INTRODUCTION

During the summer months of my youth, I could be found on most weekends exploring the wilds of the north of the Island. When I was eight my aunt and uncle moved from Onchan to Regaby, which to a townie of that age may as well have been the moon. I'd wander the country roads, either alone or with friends (whenever my aunt and uncle let a gang of us descend on their home for a few days) and I can remember seeing the huge green hand that rests atop the gatepost of Rose Cottage, a mile or so along the road from my summer retreat. It stood way above my head and I used to imagine, it being green, that it belonged to some giant Martian.

I can vaguely recall someone telling me a story of a giant whose hand the cast was based on, but as the years passed that was all I could remember. I don't know what history lessons are like today, but in the late 1970s primary school history was very basic and at secondary school we spent three years learning about ziggurats and the feudal system. No Manx history to be found, and so for many years it was just a huge green giant's hand that happened to be there for no particular reason. Yet, the fact remained; it was the hand of a giant, a magical word that conjures up fantastical settings and tales, be they about Goliath in the Bible, the fire giants of Norse mythology or Finn McCool, who legend says created the Isle of Man by taking a chunk out of Northern Ireland in a rage.

When I returned to the Island in the mid-1990s, I read a newspaper article that referenced the green hand and mentioned a certain Arthur Caley, and a gap in my knowledge was, if not filled, at least plugged. But who was this Arthur James Caley? I would later read more stories, usually containing mere highlights of the Manx Giant's life. I knew he came from around the Sulby area and went off to find his fortune, ending up in America. But that was as far as my knowledge stretched, or at least it was until I was contacted by a descendant of the Giant's, Carlton Mealin, who had spent several years researching Caley's story, collating the newspaper articles, the internet references and disproving much of what he discovered as misinterpretations. Carlton's research followed Caley from his youth in and around Sulby to his adventures in Manchester and London and onto Paris, his 'death' in the French capital and apparent resurrection on the streets of New York, where he was discovered by the legendary showman, P. T. Barnum.

It's a colourful tale, one with a dark secret at its core, and plaudits for piecing together Caley's life, or at least as much as we know of it, must go to Carlton, whose meticulous research left little to do from a writer's point of view. I've tried to bring the Manx Giant to life, and as Dr Frankenstein learned, that's something that is so much easier to do when someone else has done all the hard work and delivered the body of evidence to you.

Throughout his life, Caley collected a long list of aliases – Manx Giant, Sulby Giant, Goshen Giant, Turkish Giant, Arabian Giant, Palestine Giant, Egyptian Giant, Middlebush Giant and Colonel Routh Goshen (with variations of Ruth and Goshan) – and there is no mention of Caley with many of the references to these characters. Yet if you've heard one of these names, chances are it was a tale about Caley.

With a story that is so reliant on hearsay and snippets of information passed down through generations, it's nigh on impossible to produce an error-free biography. A prime example of this is an extract from *Giants: The Vanished Race of Mighty Men*[1], which has just three lines on Caley.

It says he grew to a height of eight feet two, was born in 1819 and that he lived with his wife – herself six feet two inches tall – at the Sulby Glen Hotel. Apart from stating that he lived in the Island, every detail is wrong. Caley was not eight feet two, he was not born in 1819 and he didn't live at the Sulby Glen Hotel. He was also married in America, and it's understood he never returned to the Island, so his wife couldn't possibly have lived at the Sulby Glen, even if he had.

Clearly, then, extracting the correct information about Caley was a challenge. With this in mind, please bear with me if a date or a name doesn't quite match up. On several occasions the research threw up the same name spelled a number of ways, as with Routh Goshen. Caley's mother was referred to as Ann and Anne, and the weathering to her gravestone doesn't help, although it looks like Ann, and that is how the Manx Sun spelled her name on the letters page when she wrote to them in 1853. Another name I can't be sure about is Cashin, or Cashen, the man who 'encouraged' Caley to leave the Island and became his manager. In both instances I've gone with the options that most seem to agree on. Likewise, there were many variations in the height and weight of Caley, although this is probably because the reports came at different points in his life. Again, I've gone for a top height and weight that would seem to fit in with the majority of references.

Ultimately, I've tried my best to do justice to Arthur Caley, both as a man and a giant, and show that his life story wasn't just another tall tale. Enjoy the read.

John Quirk,
Colby, 2009

Chapter 1

THE EARLY YEARS

When Ann Caley gave birth to her twelfth child, there had been nothing physically remarkable in her previous eleven, and nor would there be in her thirteenth, to suggest that the one who made up the dozen would be any different. Baby Arthur James must have seemed like any other child – two feet, two hands and a mouth that screamed when hungry.

Ann herself was of average stature, while her husband, also called Arthur, was considered a strapping fellow, although he was hardly immense. Yet sometimes life throws up the most peculiar of magical happenings. There was nothing unusual about Arthur Caley junior as a young lad. But at some point in his mid-teens he started to grow – and he didn't stop until, by the time he'd reached his late-twenties, he'd topped out at seven feet eleven inches and weighed in at more than four hundred pounds.

That he would become known as the Manx Giant was perhaps inevitable, but the path that his life would lead him on was anything but predictable. Given that he is one of the most notable (not to mention one of the most *noticeable*) Manxmen of the last two hundred years, there is surprisingly little known about his life story; certainly when it comes to sifting out the hard facts from the careless journalism, exaggerated half-truths and blatant untruths that distort it.

Caley was born on 16th November 1824 at a place called The Well, about one mile west of Sulby crossroads. The Giant's parents, Ann (née Kewley) and Arthur, married in Lezayre Parish Church on 7th July 1804, his paternal grandparents being John Caley and Margaret Brew, who married in May 1774. The Brew line can be traced back to Muldonny

Carlton Mealin and Billy Graham at The Well where Arthur Caley was born in 1824.

McBrew, born about 1375, who is noted in a study[2] of the Brews as being 'one of the eldest and worthiest of all the Land of Mann and Inquest to the 24 Keys', while the first generation to drop the 'Mc' was John Brew in 1565.

Most references suggest Ann, born 1780, and Arthur, born 1781, had twelve children, but this is because of the omission of a daughter, Elizabeth, who was born second – in 1806 – but about whom little is known. It's possible she died as a baby, but whatever her fate she was omitted from certain versions of the family tree.

'As a descendant, I have always known of Arthur Caley, as stories were often passed down from relatives,' Carlton explains. 'But I really became interested in 2004 when some new claims began to appear and these were strongly disputed by members of the family. During 2005, I began extensive research in an attempt to get to the bottom of it. Several meetings with Billy Graham, my great uncle, the Giant's oldest surviving relative, further convinced me that these claims were very likely untrue, as he was adamant that they contradicted what he had always been told.'

The overgrown shell of the Caley home remains today, although the ruined cottage seems ludicrously small to have been home to a giant, never mind a family with such a brood. The interior measures just twenty six feet by thirteen feet, while the ceiling height of six feet four would have caused Arthur some discomfort by the time he reached his mid-to-late teens and began to grow. It's a wonderfully tranquil place, off the beaten track, and the decrepit state of the cottage just adds to the mystique that surrounds Caley. *Rural Architecture in the North of the Isle of Man*[3] contains information and pictures of the interiors of cottages from this era and how they were used. As you enter through the front door, it's likely that the interior to the left would have had no ceiling, being open to the roof, thus allowing Caley to stand upright in this area. The other side of the cottage would have had a ceiling with loft space above, either for storage or for children to sleep, which is an arrangement that can be seen in cottages at Cregneash in the south of the Island.

According to records in the possession of the current owners of the land, the cottage at The Well was part of a 17-acre site owned by Caley's parents and the vague remains of two outbuildings near to the cottage can still be seen. Ann Caley also had a half-share in another croft, for which the location isn't known. The entire small holding at The Well, and Ann's half-share, was sold off in 1871, seven years after she had passed away, each field auctioned separately to ensure the best price. The separation of the land brought an end to the small holding, and to the Caley connection with the site, as someone from the family had lived there until the auction.

Caley's parents clearly had some standing in the area, and some money behind them, although the size of the family home suggests things weren't easy with such a large family. The cottage is barely large enough, by today's standards, for a single person. With the arrival of young Arthur, it was most likely home to mum and dad and nine youngsters, with the eldest children, John and Jane, at the time aged twenty and seventeen respectively, probably having moved out. Three years later, in 1827, it would have got even busier following the arrival of the Giant's younger sister, Catharine, the last of the Caley siblings to be born.

It was inevitable that the Giant would be drawn into farming, no doubt alongside his older brothers, and probably from a very early age. Arthur was fourteen when St Stephen's Church and School was opened in Sulby in 1838, one of eleven churches built by Bishop William Ward, but it's unlikely that the Giant received any formal education before or after St Stephen's opened. Instead, the fields around the village provided what life education Caley received, and the hard manual labour and long hours will have only helped develop him into the colossus he became.

Chapter 2

LIFE AS A GIANT

It could be argued that the prejudices of society have, in some respects, been watered down with the passing of each generation. We are, broadly speaking, more tolerant of those who might be classed as different, although certain elements of society remind us on an all too regular basis that prejudice still exists in many forms.

Today, a person standing close to eight feet tall would find many aspects of life challenging, be it difficulty in finding clothes and shoes to fit, a car to drive or the unwanted attention of those who might find that person an easy target for ridicule, such as the experiences recounted by the late Sandy Allen, the American who, at seven feet seven and one quarter inches, held the title of world's tallest woman for many years until her death in August 2008. In the biography, *Cast a Giant Shadow*[4], Sandy told of the ridicule she suffered as a child for her size and looks and how she learned to cope with that adversity.

Rewind to the first half of the nineteenth century, and one can only guess at the challenges that Caley must have faced on a daily basis. Caley was most likely a tall teenager, but it wasn't until he was seventeen that he began to take on gigantic proportions. One of the most unusual aspects about Caley was that he was a 'true giant' – the rest of his body grew in proportion to his height and he had no known defect. Giants are typically thin, or at least in proportion to their height, but Caley was a man mountain; broad-shouldered, barrel-chested, with thighs like the trunk of a Redwood. He was, by all accounts, an incredible specimen of a man. There are no medical records to explain why Caley grew so tall, but the conditions associated with gigantism usually involve an abnormality with the pituitary gland, which affects hormone imbalance, often resulting in the person being sterile. As Caley had no natural children that we know of, this may well have been the case with him. In addition to his build, Caley lived to a good age – sixty-four – which is unusual for a giant. In contrast, American Robert Pershing Wadlow, at eight feet 11.1 inches widely considered the tallest man on record, was just twenty-two when he died in 1940.

The years Caley spent working farms with his father provide the main source of the surprisingly few tales about him that have endured. Of course, all relate to him utilising his super-human strength; indeed one such story, of him lifting a cart full of turnips that had lost a wheel and replacing it single-handedly, brings to mind a young Superman lifting Jonathan Kent's van in the first Christopher Reeve movie. It's said that Caley could hold a brother in the palm of each hand and dance them around like a pair of small dolls. Another tale tells how Caley moved a rock weighing a ton into a field to give the cattle something to use as a scratching post; another that he carried a ship's anchor weighing half a ton for a mile just for a bet. It's these colourful tales that are difficult to substantiate.

'There are stories of Caley being able to lift a bag of flour with one hand and toss it around, and along with the holding of the cart to replace the wheel, I've nothing to say that these aren't true,' says Carlton. 'Looking at his size, and given the fact that he worked on farms, I imagine these may well be accurate. However, I don't think the ship's anchor rings true. There was another giant, Angus McAskill, who was very well-known at that time. There is a lot of documentation about his exploits, and there is an identical story about him carrying an anchor. McAskill was born one year after Caley, dying in 1863, and I understand he also ended up working for Barnum, so I think somewhere along the line the tale about McAskill has been mixed up with Caley.

'Uncle Billy says the Giant carried the flag at the head of the procession when they opened the Albert Tower above Ramsey, built to commemorate the visit of Prince Albert and Queen Victoria on 20th

September 1847. I tried to find a reference to that – I found the list of the procession, but there was no mention of Arthur Caley. There were three newspapers around at that time, and I checked all three. The only explanation I can think of is that the official order of procession only featured the dignitaries, and I wonder whether Caley carried the flag at the head of the general public, after the dignitaries, because it didn't name anyone else. The dates certainly fit in – the tower was opened in 1849, two years before Caley left the Island.'

For Billy, recounting tales of the Giant seems as frustrating as it is enjoyable. 'I suppose there is no reason for there to be anything on record about Caley until he reached the age of eighteen or so,' says Billy. 'He was probably just a normal tall teenager until then. He started growing when other people stopped. If I had been interested in all this as a youngster I could have asked my uncle about Caley and his life in Sulby. As time goes on, people are forgetting these stories. You know, hundreds of visitors used to get off that train [at Sulby] every day and walk to Tholt-y-Will. Some would have an idea of the Manx Giant and ask if they could see the photograph of him, and my uncle would show them Arthur's boot, too. One of his shoes was lent to the Folk Museum, and another disappeared and never came back – it's reported to have turned up in the Coniston Arms in the Lake District, although I don't know how true that is.

'Arthur was also a bouncer on the Sulby Claddaghs. They used to hold a fayre at Lezayre Church, like a mart selling animals, but the cattle smashed up the railings and the wardens suggested using the Claddaghs to stage it. When the locals were drinking too much and got a bit rowdy, Caley would be there as bouncer, along with some of his brothers. He would have been just the job as a bouncer!'

Word of a giant from the north was slowly spreading, as was evidenced by a report in the *Manx Sun*[5] in September 1848, following an appearance by Caley in Douglas:

MANX GIANT – On Friday morning last, the promenaders of Douglas Pier had their nerves somewhat shaken by the sudden

MANX GIANT.—On Friday morning last the promenaders of Douglas Pier had their nerves somewhat shaken by the sudden apparition of a giant gravely stalking amongst them, and yet apparently enjoying the lively scene of the departing mail steamer with a zest no whit behind that of his pigmy neighbours. This stalwart descendant of Anak turned out to be a youth from the parish of Ballaugh, named Arthur Caley. He stands 7 feet and 1 inch in height, though only 20 years of age, is stout in proportion, and amazingly powerful. He has a brother who exceeds him in height, bulk, and strength.

Cutting from the Manx Sun of 1848 describing Caley's visit to Douglas.

apparition of a Giant gravely stalking amongst them, and yet apparently enjoying the lively scene of the departing mail steamer with a zest no whit behind that of his pigmy neighbours. This stalwart descendant of Anak turned out to be a youth from the parish of Ballaugh, named Arthur Caley. He stands 7 feet 1 inch in height, though only 20 years of age, is stout in proportion, and amazingly powerful. He has a brother who exceeds him in height, bulk, and strength.

The journalist clearly employed a spot of poetic licence, although who's to say that Caley wasn't averse to knocking a few years off his age – he would have been twenty three at the time – and dazzling the public and media with tales of a more imposing brother back at home.

At some point around 1850, Ann Caley and her family moved from The Well to a house next to where the Sulby Glen Hotel would be built, on the corner of the Clenagh Road. It's not clear when the move occurred – Arthur Caley senior had died in 1847, aged sixty-five, and it was thought the move came shortly after. However, the census of 1851 shows the Caleys still living at The Well on Curragh Road. Carlton believes there may have been an error on the census, as they were definitely at the new home before Caley left the Island mid-1851 and it is thought he lived in that house for at least a year. When the Caleys

The cottage next to the Sulby Hotel. The previous cottage on this site is where Arthur and his family are thought to have moved to in the late 1840s. Caley left the Island shortly afterwards and the Sulby Hotel, which had not yet been built, was never lived in by him. The popular idea that the tall doors inside the hotel were to accommodate him is a myth.

moved to the house it faced east, but it was later rebuilt – thought to have been overseen by Arthur's youngest sibling, Catharine, sometime after 1867 – as south-facing, overlooking the Sulby Straight.

For many years it was believed that Caley had lived at the Sulby Glen Hotel, which has remarkably high doorways thought to have been designed specifically for the Giant. As nice a tale as it is, particularly for a pub landlord to spin to punters, the height of the doors had nothing to do with Caley – an ordnance survey map of the area in 1870 shows the hotel hadn't been built at that stage.

Just to the west of where the Sulby Glen now stands was another public house, the Glen Mooar Inn. Caley turned twenty-six in 1850 and still hadn't reached his full height. His mother would often be found in the Glen Mooar enlisting the help of customers and staff to help move

The grave of Arthur Caley senior in Lezayre churchyard.

the Giant, who was confined to his bed with severe growing pains, an experience borne out by the accounts of other giants. Other stories have Caley living for a while at Glen Mooar Inn but these can't be substantiated – given the fact that he was struggling with incredible pain at the time, it's possible that he may have become bed-ridden on occasion while sampling the wares in the Glen Mooar.

The over-elaboration of stories involving Caley continued over the years, even long after his death. In 1947, the *Isle of Man Daily Times* ran an article[6] that claimed Caley was Britain's biggest ever giant, stood eight feet two inches and weighed forty-six stone in his prime. It features many of the tales about Caley, including the ship's anchor, but is riddled with inaccuracies, including the exaggerated height and weight and a wrong date of birth. It does, however, suggest what Caley's daily menu may have been like; usually porridge for breakfast, with fish and potatoes for dinner, and sometimes beef with broth, made of shelled barley, cabbage, leeks, onions, potatoes and parsley mashed up together.

The entrance to Rose Cottage in Regaby which has an iron cast of Caley's hand on the top one of its gateposts. From the tip of the middle fingr to the ground is exactly 7"11", the height Caley was widely regarded to have grown to in maturity.

The report claimed that Caley was remembered by an 82-year-old woman, Helena Tupper, to whom several references are attributed. It also mentions Catherine Graham, Billy's mother, who lived at the house next to the Sulby Glen Hotel, and how Catherine had been told stories of Ann Caley having to reach her arms above her head to get her hands into her son's pockets. None of these stories are attributed to Catherine, however, but, seemingly, to Mrs Tupper. This is where huge holes appear in the article, and why it's difficult to lend any weight to its contents. Interestingly, it claims men came from England looking to exploit Caley, who, 'cautious and distrustful of foreigners', lent a more ready ear to the advice of an unnamed uncle, who used 'subtle flattery' to appeal to Caley's vanity, which may have some basis in truth. But

A pair of Caley's boots held in the Manx Museum.
They are fifteen inches long and six inches wide, though he was not fully grown
when these were made.

more of Mrs Tupper later.

The lack of documentation about Caley's years in the Island leaves question marks over several matters, including the huge green hand on the pillar of Rose Cottage in Regaby. It's said to be a cast of Caley's hand and from ground level to the finger tips the distance is seven feet eleven inches. There were, in fact, two right hands, one on each of the original gateposts. According to the current owners of the cottage, John and Joan Callow, the right-hand gatepost was knocked down in the early 1950s by a lorry, carrying fuel for the boiler house, when reversing into the garden. The hand that was attached to said gatepost disappeared and hasn't been heard of since, while the gatepost wasn't replaced in order to leave room for future visits by the lorry.

It's not clear who had the casts made in the first place. The cottage was home to a market garden for many years and at the time that Caley was 'growing', the owners, according to Sally McCambridge in her book, *Andreas*[7], were Thomas and Mary Harrison, who took over at the cottage in 1844. They left in 1852, a year after Caley had left the Island, and the cottage changed hands several times in subsequent years. A name connected with the casts of the Giant's hands was Captain George Burrows, who McCambridge has as a tenant at the cottage between 1903 and his death in 1914. The assumption had always been that Burrows had employed Caley prior to his departing the Island, but this is wide of the mark as Burrows wasn't born until 1846.

In her 1800-1914 history of Ramsey, *Shining by the Sea*[8], Constance Radcliffe records blacksmith John Clague as owning a foundry in the town in 1863 and producing iron goods of all sorts, including all the ornamental iron-work on Ramsey's Queen's Pier and 'a model of the right hand of the Sulby Giant, Arthur Caley, still to be seen at Rose Cottage'. The casts were, it would seem, made at some point after 1863, which doesn't rule Burrows out as the man who commissioned them, although it's not clear what the link between the two men might have been.

McCambridge mentions Frank Callow of Rose Cottage, John's father, who bought the cottage in the 1930s from William Lord, and she reports that a resident of Andreas recalled that Frank Callow was brother-in-law to Arthur S Clague, whose family ran John Clague & Son ironmongery. Casts of the hand, says McCambridge, would have been produced as a novelty item, perhaps with tourists in mind. While not stated in the book, the suggestion seems to be that Frank Callow had the casts fitted to the gateposts at Rose Cottage. However, John Callow doesn't think this theory rings true, doubting that his father would have been involved and believing it more likely to have happened pre-1900.

Whatever the truth, a few casts of Caley's hands have survived the years, with four on display in the Manx Museum and another in private ownership in Lezayre, while reports of others have surfaced from time to time, including one that a cast was at one time attached to a wall behind the Isle of Man Bank in Ramsey.

The Manx Museum is also home to a pair of Caley's leather boots –

An iron cast of Caley's hand donated to the Manx Museum in 2006 by an American, Nancy Smith. It has a silver plate, which pulls out to reveal a small nook in the back of the hand. The plate bears the inscription: 'A model of the late Arthur Kaley's hand. The Manx Giant stood 7' 8" aged 22 years'.

fifteen inches long and six inches wide – and Billy owns a single shoe that belonged to the Giant. The leather boots were donated to the museum by Mrs Lord in February 1931 – the wife of William, owner of Rose Cottage at the time. There is, therefore, some deeper link between Caley and Rose Cottage than is known. Not only did the gateposts bear casts of his hands, but someone at the cottage between 1851 and 1931 had acquired a pair of the Giant's boots. Was it Caley himself who had the link to the cottage, perhaps working for the Harrisons before leaving the Island? Or was it one of the owners or tenants, in the years after he left, who had a link to Caley, either as a friend of the Giant's or, as is perhaps more likely, his family?

The first donations for the museum's Caley collection arrived in 1922; an iron cast of his hand, courtesy of a Mrs Corlett, and a silhouette portrait of the Giant, donated by a Mrs Christian. The second iron cast was acquired from Kate Morrison in 1952 and the third was part of original displays at Castle Rushen, origin unknown.

The Caley display is housed in a glass case in the Lower Folk Gallery, a fitting location as the room has a somewhat dark and mysterious feel to it. As intriguing as the exhibits are, it's a shame there's nothing more to depict such a fascinating character than a few iron casts and a pair of boots. The most interesting of the items is the latest acquisition, another iron cast of Caley's hand donated in 2006 by an American, Nancy Smith, from a collection owned by her late husband, Dr James Smith. It has a silver plate, which pulls out to reveal a small nook in the back of the hand, the plate bearing the inscription: 'A model of the late Arthur Kaley's hand. The Manx Giant stood 7' 8" aged 22 years'. The inscription suggests that the cast was made after Caley was reported dead in Paris, which points to the cast having been made in the Isle of Man, although the misspelling of his surname is curious; the engraver has spelled the name as it sounds, and an engraver from the Island would have known how to spell Caley.

Dr Smith collected penny arcade games, fairground amusements and carnival memorabilia and it is thought he picked the hand up at an auction of items that once belonged to a member of the Roosevelt family. The purpose of the small recess in the hand is difficult to ascertain – there is a ring on the base of the hand, which suggests it may have hung from something, although that seems impractical – if it was the case, as soon as the plate was opened the contents would spill out. Another possibility is that the hand stood upright, perhaps chained to a bar, and contained snuff for the enjoyment of punters.

Of all the missing links surrounding Caley's younger years, perhaps the most intriguing piece of the jigsaw is the identity of the man who persuaded him to leave the Island, a man by the name of Cashin. It's known they left together, but who Cashin was and how the Giant knew him are questions without solid answers. The 'uncle' theory is a common one, mentioned both in the *Isle of Man Daily Times* article of 1947 and again in a 1958 article in the *Ramsey Courier*[9], a report that also referenced several of the tales from Caley's childhood, including lifting the cart and carrying the anchor. The fact that the article also contained several inaccuracies, including the wrong name for his mother, makes it difficult to give its contents any credence, similar to the problem with the *Daily Times* account, which even suggested that Caley exhibited in England under the stage name of McAskill, which is clearly untrue.

However, there is more corroborative evidence of a family link. In an Isle of Man Family History Society journal, Caley is mentioned in a February 1852 letter from a James Cashin in Australia to his wife Ann (née Teare), who was living in the Isle of Man, urging her to follow him to the goldfields while he sought his fortune. James wrote[10]: 'You speak of William, and that he is making his fortune with Caley [the Manx Giant], but perhaps I may have an independency made here before you arrive.'

Given the manner in which James refers to William, the inference is that he is another Cashin. Furthermore, Carlton has a copy of a will that mentions a William Cashin and wife Anne Cashin, along with Arthur's sister, Catharine. However, the will states that Anne Cashin was the granddaughter of Arthur Caley senior – meaning she was the Giant's niece. This is feasible, if she was the daughter of one of the Giant's elder siblings, who married Cashin; not an uncle, therefore, more a 'nephew-in-law' who was older than his uncle, but it is easy to see how confusion may have arisen.

Other family tales suggest Caley wasn't a willing accomplice of Cashin. 'There is a story that Caley was forcibly removed from the Island,' says Carlton. 'But how would you kidnap a man of Caley's stature, other than at gunpoint? Other theories speculate that he was blackmailed into leaving, but there is nothing to substantiate this.'

Another suggestion passed down the years was that the Giant may have been 'slow', and in a letter to the *Manx Sun*[11], after his death had been reported in Paris, Ann Caley claimed her son had been duped into

THE MANX GIANT.—The inhabitants of Liverpool would doubtless be much surprised to see yesterday walking up and down our streets a man of extraordinary dimensions. The person to whom we allude is Arthur Caley, a giant, from Sulby, Lezayre, Isle of Man. He is only twenty-three years of age, stands seven feet three inches high, and weighs twenty-one stones. He is a Manx farmer, and has a little property of his own. He arrived in Liverpool yesterday morning by the King Orry, Captain Quayle, from Douglas. He comes to bid farewell to a number of his neighbours and friends, who are about to emigrate. We understand he is to visit the Sailors' Home Bazzar to-day, where he will, no doubt, be an object of great interest.—*Mercury* of Friday.

An article in the Manx Sun describing Caley's arrival in Liverpool.

leaving. However, looking at the evidence from his later years in the USA, it's not a theory that holds up. In the letter to the *Manx Sun*, Ann said Arthur had been taken from the Island 'contrary to my wishes and without my consent'. Whatever the circumstances, it's clear that she did not approve of Caley teaming up with Cashin, regardless of whether or not he was a member of the family.

So why did Caley leave the Island? Was he in fact Cashin's 'uncle', or merely a friend? Was he forced to leave by some means, or was it a genuine desire to seek his fame and fortune among the freak shows and circuses? Or perhaps Caley felt too self-conscious in such a small community and sought refuge among other extraordinary people. Whatever the reasons, Caley packed his bags in the summer of 1851 and left the Island with Cashin. The date isn't known, but there is a reference in the *Mercury* newspaper in Liverpool to Caley arriving in the city in early May, although the account suggests he was planning on returning to the Island. The report was reproduced in the *Manx Sun*[12]:

THE MANX GIANT - The inhabitants of Liverpool would doubtless be much surprised to see yesterday walking up and down our streets a man of extraordinary dimensions. The person to whom we allude is Arthur Caley, a Giant from Sulby, Lezayre,

Isle of Man.

He is only twenty three years of age, stands seven feet three inches high, and weighs twenty one stones. He is a Manx farmer, and has a little property of his own.

He arrived in Liverpool yesterday morning by the King Orry, from Douglas. He comes to bid farewell to a number of his neighbours and friends, who are about to emigrate. We understand he is to visit the Sailors Home Bazaar today, where he will, no doubt, be an object of great interest.

Did Caley return to the Island before leaving again later in the summer? Or was the trip to Liverpool to bid farewell to those emigrating merely a ruse to throw his mother and family off the scent? Either way, the Giant left behind his family and friends. If Ann Caley was upset that her son was gone, she would likely have been distraught if she'd known that she would never see him again. Yet that is how events transpired; it's understood Caley never returned to his roots and Ann died in 1864, her final resting place being in Lezayre Churchyard alongside her husband.

The *Daily Times* claimed Caley did return, at the age of fifty-six – that would be 1875 going by his date of birth in the article – with Mrs Tupper saying she remembered him well. A young girl at the time, Caley would bounce her on his knee and regale her with stories of the circus. But none of this is attributed to Catherine Graham, and there is no record of such a return home within Caley's family. Another hole in the *Daily Times* report is that it claims Caley 'stayed with his brother, Charles Caley, who farmed the Creig, St Jude's'. The Giant, however, didn't have a brother called Charles.

He may not have returned home, but Caley's exploits would not be forgotten. Manxman Clucas Joughin featured Caley as one of two giant heroes in his 1903 novel, *Gorry, Son of Orry*[13], a children's adventure story of smugglers, Redcoats and Manx nationalistic fervor, with a young hero descended from the legendary Viking King of Mann.

Chapter 3

A YOUNG MAN'S DESTINY

Freak shows existed, in one form or another, centuries before Caley left Manx shores but it was the Victorian era which saw them firmly established as a serious money-making form of entertainment. Whatever the reasons and circumstances for Caley heading to England with Cashin, money will have played a major part. A man of Caley's stature would have had freak show owners clamouring to secure his services, a fact that Cashin, as his manager, must have quickly realised.

In the United States, a showman by the name of Phineas Taylor Barnum was already firmly established as one of the leading exponents of exploiting both the exhibits in his New York museum and the paying public, whose curiosity seemed to know no bounds. By 1846, Barnum had more than 400,000 punters a year passing through his doors, there to view the albinos, midgets and giants, who were mixed with models of cities and a colourful menagerie, introduced to complement the older display of stuffed animals.

In Britain, and indeed throughout Europe, it was the time of the entrepreneur, with the popularity of freak shows ever increasing, no doubt helped by Barnum's tour of Europe with General Tom Thumb – Charles Stratton, the 'Smallest Man Who Ever Walked Alone' – in 1844-45, during which he met Queen Victoria. Dwarfs such as Major Mite and Harold Pyatt became regular attractions in travelling exhibitions, appearing in music halls and fairs, and into this mix walked Arthur Caley, who first made his mark in Manchester and around the North West.

Manchester was a mill town (it would receive city status two years after Caley's stay), with a population of 186,000 producing wool, silk and cotton. The first report of the Giant being exhibited was in the

REDUCTION OF PRICES. — MODEL OF ROME; size, 588 square feet. — This splendid Work of Art yet ON VIEW in the Exchange Rooms of this town, entrance om Ducie-street. — Open from eleven to five o'clock, and from even to nine p.m. Lectures at twelve, three, and eight p.m. Morning Exhibition, 1s.; Evening ditto, 6d Schools and children under twelve years of age half-price.

FREE-TRADE HALL.—DAY EXHIBITION. NOTICE.—The beautiful Moving DIORAMA of OUR NATIVE LAND, or ENGLAND AND THE SEASONS. y Messrs. Grieve, William Telbin, and John Absolon; the animals y J. F. Herring, senior, from the Gallery of Illustration, Regent-street, London, will be EXHIBITED EACH DAY DURING HIS WEEK, at two o'clock. Admission: Reserved seats, 2s.; children, half-price: body of all, 1s.—In the evening, at eight o'clock: Reserved seats, 1s; children, half-price: body of hall and gallery, 6d.

FREE-TRADE HALL. — Every Evening, a Beautiful Series of SCENIC ILLUSTRATIONS, entitled OUR NATIVE LAND, OR ENGLAND & THE SEASONS. hose pictures are painted by the celebrated artists, Messrs Grieve, William Telbin, and John Absolon; the animals by J. F. Herring, senior, (the gentlemen who have produced the most successful of modern dioramas,—"The Overland Route to India,") hey have been exhibited since the month of January last, at the Gallery of Illustration, Regent-street, London, from whence they re removed direct to the Free-trade Hall, and will be found superior to anything of the kind that has yet visited the provinces. The music selected and arranged by Dr RIMBAULT. Organist—Mr. G. HUMPHRIES. Admission: In the evening, reserved seats, 1s.; children, half-price; body of hall and gallery, 6d.—Day exhibition, reserved seats, 2s.; children, half-price; body of hall, 1s.

WILL be EXHIBITED, on Friday and Saturday next, the 4th and 5th July, and the following eek, at the Exchange Room, Manchester (entrance from Exchange-street), the Young MANX GIANT, being the tallest man nown in the world, and the most proportionate giant ever exhibited. He is the son of a respectable farmer in the Isle of Man, nd worked upon the farm up to a very recent period. He tands seven feet six inches high, is 22 years of age, and may yet e considered as a boy as regards his full growth, having during he last twelve months grown fully three inches. His bone and

A notice in the Manchester Guardian advertising the appearance of Caley along with other exciting exhibits such as a model of Rome and a series of beautiful scenic illustrations.

Manchester Guardian[14], the first incarnation of today's *Guardian*. The notice read:

Will be exhibited, on Friday and Saturday next, the 4th and 5th of July, and the following week, at the Exchange Room, Manchester (entrance from Exchange Street), the Young Manx Giant, being the tallest man known in the world and the most proportionate giant ever exhibited. He is the son of a respectable farmer in the Isle of Man and worked upon the farm up to a very recent period. He stands seven feet six inches high, is twenty two years of age [he was actually four years older], and may yet be considered as a boy as regards his full growth, having during the last twelve months grown fully three inches. His bone and muscle is of a most Herculean nature and his strength without parallel. Admission, from eleven am to five pm, one shilling; ditto from six to nine pm, 6d.

The reference to his height, and the fact that he was still growing, may explain the general discrepancies in reports of Caley's height, certainly if he was still growing aged twenty seven.

The next account in the *Guardian*[15] came three days later:

A Manx Giant – There is at present exhibiting, in one of the Exchange rooms, an extraordinary specimen of humanity, in the person of Arthur Caley, who is the son of a Manx farmer, and was born at Lazare, about five miles from Ramsay. Although only in his 22nd year, Caley is seven feet six inches high, weighs 21 stone 8lbs and is altogether well proportioned. We mentioned a visit Caley paid to Manchester and the neighbourhood a short time since; he intended to visit other towns, not exhibiting himself; but he is said to have suffered so much annoyance from the crowds who followed him whenever he appeared in the streets, that he was compelled to desist from walking there, and has since been exhibiting himself in Liverpool, Wigan, St Helens, Ormskirk, and other places. It is said that Caley has grown fully three inches within the last twelve months, however this may be, his present gigantic procerity, and great muscular development, seem to render him as monstrous a specimen of the capability of development possessed by the human species, as any that has been seen for some ages.

This provides an insight into the attention Caley must have drawn. If part of his reasoning for leaving the Isle of Man was to escape such scrutiny, he would have soon realised it was going to be no better elsewhere. What's clear is that Caley (or perhaps Cashin) was happy to play on his humble, working-class roots, perhaps hoping that the quirkiness – and, at the time, relative obscurity – of the Island would intrigue the public, although the 'tallest man known in the world' line would do the trick on its own.

A week later, the same paper[16] ran another notice:

> The Manx Giant – After Bradley, the Yorkshire giant, long since dead, and O'Brien, the Irish giant, still longer defunct, and who was certainly the greatest man (in stature) of whom in modern times we have heard, comes the young Manx giant, now exhibiting in the Exchange Room, Exchange Street... He is well-proportioned, and, judging from his hand and joints, we should say of strength proportionate to his stature.... Can this Arthur Caley be a descendant of one of the old Norse Vikings, who long ruled in the Isle of Man, and of whose great stature skalds have sung and sages told strange stories? It is curious that although neither his parents nor brothers exceed the ordinary height (nor did his immediate ancestors), there is a tradition in the family of some remoter 'forbear' being a giant in the old time. These reproductions of personal peculiarities, after a lapse of generations, are amongst some of the most curious physiological phenomena. Meanwhile, as Arthur is said to be growing at the rate of three inches a year, we say – go and see him before he gets so tall as to be quite out of sight.

More interesting snippets of information and speculation are revealed; there's no record of any distant relative of Caley being a giant, and this was probably a touch of poetic licence, either from the *Guardian* or Cashin.

There's another mention[17] of Caley four days later, on July 16th, in a letter to the editor, the writer suggesting that a giant of Lancashire, John Middleton, born in 1578, was deserving of a mention alongside 'the wonderful Manx Giant', Bradley and O'Brien. Middleton, apparently, stood an impressive nine feet three inches, which would have put him just six inches shy of Goliath.

Caley remained in Manchester and the North West during the summer and notices in the *Guardian*[18] have him exhibiting in September during the Belle Vue Wakes. The mention of Caley is brief, but the notices give an idea of the kind of circles in which the Giant worked. The notices read:

> The Proprietor of the Zoological Gardens, Belle Vue, Hyde Road, begs respectfully to announce that the above annual feast will commence on Monday, September 8th, for which he has concluded arrangements with several artists of celebrity in order to add a further attraction to the numerous interesting objects already in the gardens. The following may be enumerated:
>
> The Ethair Family, the celebrated gymnastic artists, from Franconi's, Paris; Mr Betts, with his performing dog; Mr Stonette, the unrivalled clown, from Franconi's Free-trade Hall, with his wonderful performing dogs, Hector and Ajax.
>
> On Wednesday, September 10th, Messrs Matthews and Harrison, in a grand aquatic tournament on the lake. The Manx Giant, twenty two years of age, and seven feet six inches in height, will promenade the garden daily, from the 7th to the 14th, both days inclusive.
>
> On Monday, Wednesday and Saturday, a grand display of fireworks will terminate the proceedings. Admission during the week, sixpence.

Caley's final appearance in the *Guardian*[19] was on the penultimate day of the Belle Vue Wakes, which mentioned the same acts as the previous notices.

From Manchester, Caley moved south, with Cashin in tow. There's no record of when this happened, but by early January 1852 Caley was in London, where he continued to find work in exhibits, human curiosity for 'oddities' being what it was. A popular draw for entrepreneurs of the time was exhibiting Africans, and other races considered 'exotic' in that era, brought to Britain by explorers. Today, such acts would be considered morally offensive, but the Victorian public's fascination proved a money-spinner and Caley would have been on the bill alongside them.

Unfortunately, no newspaper records of Caley's stay in London could be found and there is no anecdotal evidence either. What is known, however, is that it was a short stay, as Caley and Cashin soon packed their bags and were on the move again. Was it a lack of work that led them to head for Paris, or had Caley gone down a storm in London and been enticed to France? Whatever the reason, the Giant's name was appearing in Parisian newspaper reports by the end of January, and it was in the French capital that the Giant's story took a dark twist.

Chapter 4

DARK DEEDS IN PARIS

Paris in the early 1850s was a city in flux. By order of Napoleon III, the city was being reshaped under the direction of Baron Haussman in a bid to remove the narrow streets – shown by the revolutions to be ideal for barricades – and clean up the slums. Large areas of the city were levelled, with the poor taking refuge on the outskirts, as the middle and upper class prospered in their new boulevards, parks and markets. After London, Paris was the second largest city in Europe and the population doubled in the space of twenty years and, as with London, it was into a bustling, thriving cosmopolitan centre that Arthur Caley arrived.

One of the most popular forms of entertainment for Parisians was the café-concert, which brought together food, drink and music, and a variety of other associated 'artistic' performers, although by the late 1850s their reputation had taken something of a battering, a fact that inspired a café-concert artist, Emile Mathieu, to write a book defending these establishments. Yet when Caley's huge stride hit the pavements of Paris, it was in café-concerts – including the Salle Paganini and Jardin D'Hiver – that he found an audience for his talents. Mathieu refers to another venue, the Café du Geant, as being one of the most popular café-concerts in Paris, but there is no indication as to whether the café got its name from Caley, or another giant, Henri Simon, who exhibited in the city at around the same time as the Manx Giant.

The first record[20] of Caley appearing was in the Salle Paganini on January 25th. The Paganini was located on rue de la Chausee d'Antin, in what at the time was the 2nd arrondissement of Paris, and which by all accounts had something of a notorious reputation. Several reports in *La*

Salle newspaper suggest Caley appeared at the Paganini for at least three months, until April, and *Le Siecle* has Caley appearing in May, while *La Presse* reports him appearing at the Paganini in the September.

Another report in *La Presse*[21], while not mentioning Caley, gives an insight into an evening's proceedings at the Paganini:

> Last night took place, in the Paganini Room, the annual ball thrown by the Grand-Orient, to raise money for the destitute. There was such an immense crowd that, for an hour or two, the dances had to be interrupted. The room, splendidly lit, decorated with banners from all the theatres in Paris, filled with a large number of rich and elegant guests, did not for one instant fail to present the most brilliant and animated sight. Mr Lucien Murat, recently named Grand Master of the French Masonic Order, assisted at this charity event, which produced an abundant revenue, further increased towards midnight thanks to a quest by the patronesses and commissioners of the ball.

Notices in *La Presse* talk of the appearance of 'the famous Giant Arthur Caley, the biggest ever seen', or at a masked black-tie ball, 'the famous Scottish Giant', as he was often billed – most probably because more Parisians and visitors could point to Scotland on a map than the Isle of Man. The novelty of having someone of Caley's stature wasn't lost on those who hired him; another report[22] had him handing out bonbons at a children's ball.

At some point around this time a man called Etienne Lefevre entered Caley's circle. How they met, or indeed the exact nature of their acquaintance, isn't known, although as will become clear they grew close, be it in business, as friends, or both. While Cashin remained as Caley's manager, Lefevre was probably instrumental in securing work for the Giant. He may also have introduced Caley to the woman whose heart he would capture, a woman whom Lefevre mentioned in a later letter to Ann Caley.

Lefevre didn't name the woman. However, in the Bibliothèque Nationale de France there is a book by Adolphe Joly[23] *A la memoire du colosse de Rhodes. Le Geant Ecossaise, Sir Arthur Caley*, published in 1852, which translates *To the memory of the colossus of Rhodes. The Scottish Giant… Sir Arthur Caley*. It contains the following passage:

A Colossal Love

(spoken) – Ladies and Gentlemen, spectators, pity the spectacle before you! I have really changed, have I not? Love, a love without hope, has destroyed my feeble heart, this burning heart that consumes me from within. The roses of my cheeks are blanched; I am peaked like a two-way mirror! This is how I feel, that this beautiful adolescent will never share my fire; this is what I suffer in the constant response to my words of tenderness, this phrase that I haven't found in the Nouvelle Heloise[24]: GIVE ME SOME BRAD, IF YOU PLEASE!

He is a very big man
Lined in green velvet
In winter:
It's Caley that we name him…
All Paris wants to see
Each night
The drum major
All adorned in gold
Ah! What a pleasure I have
In admiring, in contemplating, this superb giant!!

Me, I like his expression,
His majestic air,
His big eyes,
His enormous neck,
His hide breeches,
His hat,
Sir Caley attracts me,
I like, it's a fact,
Yes, it's a top fact,
All to the top, to the top of Caley!

This beautiful bachelor
Deprived of descendants
Wants (they say)
In order to divert himself
To take a wife in Paris,
What a thought!
Caley so aloof,
Will be sought after
Then one night kidnapped
AS he is too well brought up.

Incomparably large
Accept from tomorrow
This hand…
My incurable heart
That your look tears apart,
Will be cured,
Become my darling
My dear little husband
Oh! Come down here to me,
If not I will take a ladder and climb up there with you!

Arthur Caley - The Manx Giant

My size mortifies me…
If only I could grow taller
And fatter!
Giant, I beg you,
Shrink yourself a little
And, zounds!
I will become yours completely
Your firm support
By a legal contract
Shrink yourself; I will be your half!

There was, no doubt, some colourful exaggeration employed in this description of her love for Caley, but it does provide us with our first impression of what an imposing character Caley must have been, to both men and women.

It is clear Caley's services were in demand. However, such was the fickle nature of his trade, that his time in the limelight was relatively short; regular patrons of these café-concerts would have demanded a fresh spectacle, with an ever-changing cast.

It is likely that this predicament played a major part in the events of late December 1852, a period which marked a major turning point in Caley's life.

It's understood that around this time Caley was insured for £2,000, which in today's money would be just shy of £200,000. The idea of insurance hadn't really caught on in France prior to this time, but an article in *La Presse*[25] that month revealed how the concept of insuring people's lives – 'so little understood in France for many years' – was finally taking root.

The article stated:

> The big advantages offered by English companies, who have been in their happiest arrangement ahead of all the demands of life, will end up being very popular in our country. One of them, the National Society, established in Paris, has already completed a number of life insurances in four years. The high morality of these

An engraving by A de Valmont published in Paris. The legend states that Arthur 'Calley' was born in England and was 23 years old.
It was available for purchase from la Salle Bonne-Nouvelle.

operations, their punctuality in filling religiously all their pledges, has given them a position that no competition can seriously attack. A fact that will prove the safety of their future transactions. An honourable professor of Paris, insured for one year, died almost suddenly in his prime; on his deathbed he paid the half-premium of his insurance, and although the company knew his position, they executed his last wishes, and the designated person was immediately paid. For two half-premiums of 242FR, he left 12,500FR.

A week after that article was published, Caley was dead, his passing reported on page two of *La Presse*[26]. The obituary read:

On the 1st January has died one of those beings who represents a trick of nature in the great human family, James Arthur Kaley, aged twenty seven years, and measuring two metres 50 centimetres [seven and a half foot]. This Giant, from a café on the Boulevard du Temple, was interesting to see next to the General Tom Pouce, than whom he was six times taller. It is believed he was born in Scotland.

On Christmas Day he appeared in Café Concert. The next day he figured in a charity event in the Winter Gardens. On Monday December 27th, he reappeared in Café Concert for the last time. On returning home he felt the effects of the illness to which he finally succumbed on January 1st. This man, believed to be a Hercules, was one of extreme weakness.

He died a bachelor and close to penniless. His funeral took place on Monday, January 3rd. As the funeral directors had neither coffin large enough, nor wagon strong enough to contain or carry the body of the Giant, it was necessary to have them specially constructed.

In February 1853, Ann Caley received a letter from Etienne Lefevre, informing her that her son was dead.

The letter paints a despicable picture of Cashin, suggesting he had taken all of Caley's earnings while making him pay for anything he needed. According to Lefevre, the Giant was 'beloved and esteemed for his amiable qualities and noble heart by all who knew him'. The Frenchman claimed to know Caley better than anyone other than

— Le 1er janvier est mort un de ces êtres qui sont comme un jeu de la nature dans la grande famille humaine, James-Arthur Kaley, âgé de vingt-sept ans; ayant la taille de 2 mètres 50 centimètres (7 pieds et demi). C'était le géant d'un café du boulevard du Temple, qu'il eût été intéressant de voir à côté du général Tom-Pouce, dont il avait six fois la taille. On croit qu'il était né en Ecosse.

Le jour de Noël il parut au café-concert. Le lendemain il alla figurer au Jardin-d'Hiver dans une fête de bienfaisance. Le lundi 27, il reparut au café-concert, c'était la dernière fois. Rentré chez lui il se sentit atteint de la maladie à laquelle il a succombé le 1er janvier. Cet homme, qu'on eût cru un hercule, était d'une faiblesse extrême.

Il est mort célibataire et à peu près sans fortune. Son convoi a eu lieu lundi 3 janvier. Comme l'administration des pompes funèbres n'avait ni cercueil, ni char pour contenir et porter le corps du géant, elle a dû en faire construire de spéciaux.

The notice in the Paris newspaper La Presse (above) announcing the death of 'James Arthur Kaley, aged 27 years' and (below) the announcement in the Manx Sun.

DEATH OF ARTHUR CALEY, THE MANX GIANT, IN PARIS. — This prodigy of human nature, who has been exhibited in various towns in England, and in the city of London, during the time of the memorable "Great Exhibition," died in Paris on Saturday, January 1st, 1853, where he had been exhibited for a considerable time. It appears from what is currently reported at his native place, (Sulby, Lezayre,) that he had been engaged for twelve months for exhibition, by a Parisian company, and that they had insured his life for £2,000.

Cashin and an unnamed woman with whom the Giant had 'formed an attachment':

Paris 8th February 1853

Madam – I trust you will excuse the liberty I take in writing to you on a subject which I fear will add to the grief a mother must feel for the loss of a son, who was beloved and esteemed for his amiable qualities and noble heart by all who knew him. Being intimately acquainted with him, I knew all his private affairs, better than anyone except Cashen and the lady for whom he had formed an attachment. I should be failing in any duty towards my lamented friend were I not to acquaint you with the abominable treatment he met with from Cashen. Poor Caley was so much

35

attached to Cashen and had so much confidence in him, that he gave him all his earnings, but Cashen, not content with that, made him pay for his clothing, cabs, and everything he wished for; he was so partial to him that Cashen's will was his, and anyone who offended Cashen offended him. When Caley got acquainted with the lady above mentioned, Cashen was furious against him, fearing she might open his eyes to the shameful conduct towards him. When the poor fellow was taken ill, he refused taking apartments for him in the country, as doctors had ordered. Accusing him of laziness, and threatening to use main force to oblige him to exhibit himself. A week before he died, Cashen told my uncle, to whom Caley owed 150 Francs for clothing, that he was much better, and that it was only idleness on his part; in fact he said everything he could behind his back against him, and I may say he hastened his death through his ill treatment.

The kind lady he was so much attached to sat up every night with him, and Cashen only called to see him in the afternoon. I was present at his death on the 1st January, his last breath was scarcely out of his body when Cashen took possessions of his watch, ring and eight francs, the only money he had; the watch worth 400 francs, and the ring 80, were sold for 140 francs to pay for his funeral. Cashen stating that Caley had sent all his money to his friends, &c, in England and that he should be obliged to write to his wife for money to pay his expenses back to England. Everybody was disgusted with his behavior, and was persuaded that he had not acted honestly towards the deceased. Had it not been for the gentleman with whom poor Caley was engaged, who was kind enough to pay part of his funeral, he would have been buried like a pauper; not even a clergymen called to read prayers over the grave; the same person who paid part of his funeral discharged that duty in the presence of a number of friends who followed him on to his last abode, and has had some beautiful lines written on his tomb.

I send you my address and will greatly obliged by your acquainting me with the receipt of this letter, and any information I can give you on this unfortunate affair, I shall be most happy to

THE MANX GIANT.

To the EDITOR of the MANX SUN.

SIR,—Being aware that you are always most anxious to advocate the cause of the widow and the fatherless, I most humbly implore you to bestow a small space in your valuable journal for the insertion of the following letter, which I have received from Paris, touching the death and the shameful manner in which my son, Arthur Caley, *alias* the Manx Giant, was treated by Mr. Cashen, after having been induced by him to leave a peaceable home, contrary to my wishes and without my consent.

I beg to remain, Sir, your obdt. and humble servant,
Lezayre, Feb. 23, 1853. ANN CALEY.

Paris, 8th February, 1853.

MADAM,—I trust you will excuse the liberty I take in writing to you on a subject, which I fear will add to the grief a mother must feel for the loss of a son, who was beloved and esteemed for his amiable qualities and noble heart by all who knew him. Being intimately acquainted with him, I knew all his private affairs, better than any one except Cashen and the lady for whom he had formed an attachment. I should be failing in my duty towards my lamented friend were I not to acquaint you with the abominable treatment he met with from Cashen. Poor Caley was so much attached to Cashen, and had so much confidence in him that he gave him all his earnings, but Cashen not content with that made him pay for his clothing, cabs, and everything he wished for; he was so partial to him that Cashen's will was his, and any one who offended Cashen offended him. When Caley got acquainted with the lady above mentioned, Cashen was furious against him, fearing she might open his eyes to his shameful conduct towards him. When the poor fellow was taken ill he refused taking apartments for him in the country, as the doctors had ordered. Accusing him of laziness, and threatening to use main force to oblige him to exhibit himself. A week before he died, Cashen told my uncle, to whom Caley owed 150 francs for clothing, that he was much better, and that it was only idleness on his part; in fact he said everything he could behind his back against him, and I may say he hastened his death through his ill treatment.

The kind lady he was so much attached to sat up every night with him, and Cashen only called to see him in the afternoon. I was present at his death on the 1st January, his last breath was scarcely out of his body when Cashen took possession of his watch, ring, and eight francs, the only money he had; the watch worth 400 francs, and the ring 80, were sold for 140 francs to pay his funeral. Cashen stating that Caley had sent all his money to his friends, &c., in England, and that he should be obliged to write to his wife for money to pay his expenses back to England. Everybody was disgusted with his behaviour, and was persuaded that he had not acted honestly towards the deceased. Had it not been for the gentleman with whom poor Caley was engaged, who was kind enough to pay part of his funeral, he would have been buried like a *pauper;* not even was a clergyman called to read prayers over his grave; the same person who paid part of his funeral discharged that duty in the presence of a number of friends who followed him to his last abode, and has had some beautiful lines written on his tomb.

I send you my address and will feel greatly obliged by your acquainting me with the receipt of this letter, and any information I can give you on this unfortunate affair, I shall be most happy to do so.

I remain, Madam, your most obedient servant,
ETIENNE LEFEVRE.

My address is Mons. Etienne Lefevre, chez Mons. Boussart, Tailleur, No. 5, Rue de Filles, St. Thomas, à Paris.

The letter published in the Manx Sun on 12th March 1853 from Ann Caley revealing the description of her son's death in Paris as relayed to her by Etienne Lefevre. She also expressed her great disquiet at how Cashin had originally enticed her son to leave the Island. The mystery of who Lefevre actually was continues: No. 5 Rue de Filles no longer stands.

do so.

> I remain, Madam, your most obedient servant
> Etienne Lefevre

Ann Caley's sadness at losing her son was matched only by her feelings of disgust for the way Cashin had treated him. On 23rd February, she sent Lefevre's letter to the *Manx Sun*, which printed it along with the following note:

> Sir – being aware that you are always most anxious to advocate the cause of the widow and the fatherless, I must humbly implore you to bestow a small space in your valuable journal for the insertion of the following letter, which I have received from Paris, touching the death and the shameful manner in which my son, Arthur Caley, alias the Manx Giant, was treated by Mr Cashen, after having been induced by him to leave a peaceable home, contrary to my wishes and without my consent.

This, then, is evidence that Caley may have been coerced into leaving the Island, although 'induce' can be taken in several contexts. There's nothing to suggest force; it's more likely that a young and impressionable Caley was won over by talk of bright lights and big cities, not to mention the prospect of making money.

With no word to the contrary, Ann believed her son was dead.

However, time would show that he didn't die in Paris. Several years later, most likely in the early 1860s, the Manx Giant surfaced on the streets of New York. His subsequent life in the United States means Caley's death in Paris was staged, with the insurance undoubtedly a major factor.

In his 1901 *Manx Worthies*[27], A. W. Moore has Caley dead aged twenty four (another example of the inconsistency of reporting of the Giant's age) having died in Paris due to sumptuous living and over indulgence. Moore claimed that 'the man who engaged' Caley's services had insured his life for £2,000. But who would that have been? Cashin? Lefevre? Another party? What is known is that Caley disappeared, but that doesn't

THE LATE MANX GIANT.—Mrs. Caley, mother of Arthur Caley the Manx Giant, has sent a postscript to her letter which appeared in our columns on the 12th instant, to the effect that the statement of Cashen to M. Lefevre that Caley had sent all his money to his friends in England, was incorrect, as but one remittance of £10 was received from him by his relatives during the time he was being exhibited, namely, from February 1852 to the time of his death.

As a postscript to the 12th March letter, the Manx Sun published a clarification from Ann Caley about the money her son sent home whilst being exhibited.

answer the question of who was involved in the scam.

There are several possibilities. First, that Caley knew nothing about it and simply decided to leave Paris for America, a decision which prompted Cashin to take advantage. If this was the case, it would seem Lefevre was involved too and that the letter to Ann Caley was part of an intricate plan.

The second possibility was that Caley was in cahoots with Cashin. Realising that his popularity was on the wane, Caley may have agreed to fake his death in return for a cut of the money. This scenario could have unfolded with or without Lefevre's involvement; if he didn't know, the letter to Ann would have been how he genuinely thought events had unfolded. However, given the detail in the letter relating to Caley's illness, and the fact that it was played out over a period of several days, it is hard to believe that Lefevre was unaware of what was happening. Whatever the truth, given the sum involved, it was clearly an elaborate scam.

According to a postscrit to Ann's letter to the *Manx Sun* (above) the only sum of money the family ever received from Caley was just £10. If Caley was involved in faking his own death, and then left for the US without informing his family, it points to there being some ongoing domestic problem, which most likely started before he left the Island, and this would tie in with his mother being unhappy with him taking up with Cashin in the first place.

There is another story – one that exists outside the Caley family, but whose origin is unknown – that the Giant's grave in Paris was later exhumed and a huge log found where Caley's body should have resided.

The first mention of this appears to have been in that 1958 article in the *Ramsey Courier*, although it claims the supposed insurance scam took place in America, not Paris, and is in keeping with the inaccuracies within the report. Carlton and Billy have no idea where this story came from, or indeed when the exhumation was supposed to have taken place.

Research for this book in Paris has failed to locate Caley's grave, but the changes in the city over the last 150 years are such that many cemeteries have been lost and it's highly probable that Caley's supposed resting place has gone with them.

While Caley surfaced across the Atlantic, what happened to Cashin? Julian Teare, who owns part of the parcel of land at one time owned in possession of the Caley family, has researched the history of the site. He discovered that the land sale, including for The Well, was dealt with at a Chancery Court held at Castle Rushen and that a William Cashin connected with the Caleys was involved in this case, with Cashin noted as the defendant. Was this William Cashin returned from Paris? Julian's research indicates that at this point, around 1871, the court was still accepting that Arthur Caley Junior was dead, as the Giant had stood to receive a large inheritance. If this was the same William Cashin, would he have returned to the Island if he'd been involved in the insurance scam? If he was involved, it meant he kept up the pretence even in court. It also throws up the possibility that the Caley family knew Arthur was alive in America at this point and were keeping it to themselves.

And what of Lefevre? His trail went cold, or at least it did until Caley was on his deathbed, when a Lefevre – the name, if not the man – entered the Giant's story once more.

Chapter 5

THE GREATEST SHOW ON EARTH

If freak shows and the like were popular in Europe at this time, in the US one man was setting about making them must-see attractions and establishing an entire industry from them.

The moment Caley set sail for the US, it was perhaps inevitable that a man of his stature should cross the path of P. T. Barnum. It's not clear how the two became acquainted. The widely held belief is that they met in New York, although the Brooklyn Eagle[28] claimed that Barnum discovered Caley in about 1862 while travelling abroad. If this account is true, it throws up the possibility that Barnum had some involvement in bringing Caley to the States from Paris – and if this was the case, was Barnum caught up in the insurance fraud?

It's another of those major turning points in the Giant's life about which we'll never be sure. While this was happening, he was believed dead. The story of his second life in the US only came to light after his death in 1889, although yet another contradicting story appeared in *It's a Fact*[29], a book of drawings by 'Dusty' Miller, which was published in the *Isle of Man Examiner*. This account supported claims that Caley had travelled with Barnum and Bailey, but claimed he died in the US aged forty three from suspected poisoning by a rival circus.

Subsequent to these accounts, *Isle of Man Examiner* journalist Ruth Serjeant tried to unravel the mystery in a lengthy article[30] in 1962. While elements of Serjeant's piece have been shown to be wide of the mark in light of information obtained in recent years, her investigation remains the most authoritative piece of journalism on Caley's life.

Serjeant's first major piece of evidence supporting the story that

The 'Dusty' Miller feature in 'It's A Fact' published by the Examiner during the 1930s.

Caley did go to the US is a 19th-century sepia studio portrait, taken by Abraham Bogardus, a New York photographer. It shows, seated, a huge, heavy man sporting a waxed moustache and small goatee beard and dressed in a long military coat, along with braided epaulettes and a helmet topped with white plumes. The title at the bottom of the picture reads 'Colonel Ruth Goshon. Age 43 years. Weight 620lbs. Height 7ft 11inches'. Above this inscription, written in ink, are three words – 'Arthur Caley as…' and the age '43' has also been included.

Serjeant's search threw up further evidence pointing towards Caley living in the US as Colonel Routh Goshen, including an article in the *Manx Sun*[31] in 1889 – 'A Manx(?) giant's funeral' – which included a *New York Sun* account of the death of Goshen, 'Barnum's biggest giant who died on his farm near Clyde Station, New Jersey'.

The *New York Sun* report continued: 'Colonel Goshen told the

COL. RUTH GOSHON.
Age, 43 years. Weight, 620 lbs. Height, 7 feet 11 inches.
Bogardus, Photo

The portrait of Caley taken by New York photographer Abraham Bogardus.

minister (attending him) that in early life he had been a ship's carpenter and that he had wished many times he had never abandoned his trade for the show business.' It said Goshen was born a Jew and died a Christian and that he had been born on the Isle of Man and that 'almost all members of his family were in New Zealand', although there is no known family link to New Zealand, which suggests this was another elaborate tale woven by Caley.

One member of his family who certainly didn't move to New Zealand was Arthur's elder sister, Margaret, who was nine years his senior. Serjeant discovered that Margaret had emigrated to Rochester,

43

Caley posing with a normal-sized man.

New York, having married a Robert Gelling in Lezayre in 1835. It is likely, therefore, that Caley saw in Margaret an opportunity to reinvent himself in America, although it is unclear as to when he made the trip. If Caley was involved in the insurance scam, it is likely that he departed France quickly, possibly heading across the Atlantic.

The years until he met Barnum remain a mystery, but the years that followed provide the richest in terms of information about the Giant's life. It's widely acknowledged that Barnum's eyes rang up dollar bills when he looked at people. The public were a means of making money, and he rarely missed an opportunity to part them from their hard-earned wages; in marketing terms, he was a man born out of time. The quotes 'there's a sucker born every minute' and 'every cloud has a silver lining' are often attributed to Barnum, although it seems accepted today that he didn't actually utter either of these lines. One story is that, in order to keep the public moving, Barnum had signs in his exhibitions reading 'Egress this way', realising that people would think it was another exhibit, rather than another word for exit. Once outside, they'd be digging in their pockets for more cash to get back in.

In addition, many of Barnum's acts were not quite what they were reported to be; he managed to convince people that an 80-year-old woman was, in fact, 161, but they must have been pretty convincing, as the turnstiles kept clicking over. In Caley's case, Barnum gave him the stage name of Colonel Goshen and claimed the Giant was of Arabic, Egyptian or Turkish descent, because, let's face it, if you're in 19th century America, most people would have as much an idea about the location of the Isle of Man as Caley would the Holy Grail. But Arabic and Turkish? A far more exotic proposition and more likely to tempt (and convince) the paying public.

Caley's middle-eastern persona featured in a book, *Colours of Enhancement: Theater, Dance, Music, and the Visual Arts of the Middle East*[32], edited by Sherifa Zuhur. According to this book, Barnum was exhibiting Caley sometime in the 1850s, which is earlier than most references suggest they met. In a chapter called *Race, Sexuality and Arabs in American Entertainment*, writer Lori Anne Salem used Goshen as an example of how American theatre, in its widest sense, used 'fantasy races', such as Arabian acts, in the late 19th century to explore 'the complexities of "real" racial conflicts'. Salem claimed the dime shows, or curiosity shows, sold themselves as 'educational forums for studying the hierarchical ordering of plants, animals, and especially the human races that was the cornerstone of Victorian race theory', with museums hiring scientists to lecture on the uniqueness and scientific value of each curiosity. Salem suggested that, while the public would view human curiosities from America as simply 'unique' beings, they would view those from other races, such as an Arabian giant, as being representative of the curiosity of that particular race. Salem also referenced historian Robert Bogden, who said the oddity of human exhibits in these shows wasn't just down to their physical attributes, but more the way in which those attributes were displayed; on the street, Caley would have been just a tall man, but the way he was introduced, the costume he wore, the set accorded him by a particular museum or show, would see him become an amazing 'giant'. Salem clearly wasn't aware of Goshen's background. She questioned why, whether his act was a complete fabrication or not, he was portrayed as an Arabian giant, and she too suggested that, as giants were fairly common in American theatre, the Middle-Eastern angle was added for novelty value.

The source of the name Goshen is also questionable. In Isle of Man Newspapers' *Manx Millennium* supplement[33], journalist Terry Cringle credits George Broderick with revealing there were two Goshen Fields in Sulby between St Jude's and Sulby Bridge, close to where Caley lived. It would be nice to think that Caley chose the name himself as a nod to his birthplace. However, while a romantic idea, Goshen was a region of Egypt mentioned in the Bible – Joseph's stay in Egypt – and it's probable that Barnum chose the name to further enhance the background he'd created for Caley.

Barnum portrayed many of his performers as colonel, major or captain and in the case of Routh Goshen concocted colourful tales about him to support the myth, including an elaborate illustrious military career. Other stories[34] had him moving a 1,700-pound cannon and crushing the head of a grizzly bear with a rock. In a bid, no doubt, to accentuate Caley's stature, he would often perform with dwarfs – Major Atom, Commodore Nutt, General Tom Thumb and Admiral Dot were some of the best known performers of that era – and to elaborate his military credentials, Caley would wear full uniform with a huge plumed helmet, the top of which must have been close to ten feet from the floor.

The various ploys worked. The Giant went on show and the crowds queued up to see him. By the 1870s, Barnum was billing Goshen as the 'largest living man' and newspaper adverts had him sharing – and often topping – the bill with humorist Billy Reeves, the 'Renowned Hibernian Boys' Connor and Bradley, gymnasts Williams and Mankin, the 'Great, the Brilliant, the Fascinating, the Original Female Minstrels', comedians Billy Hart and James Maas, and General Grant Junior, along with something called 'The Goshen speciality – A kiss in the dark'. Quite who Caley was kissing is a mystery, but one can only assume a ladder was involved at some point during the act. Joining the collection of unusual exhibitions was a menagerie of wild beasts and, after an absence of nine years, the celebrated 'Madagascar Family', who were albinos brought to the US by Barnum and introduced at his American Museum in New York.

Understanding what made Barnum tick helps enhance the picture of what life would have been like for Caley, and as a starting point there are few places better than the Barnum Museum in Connecticut[35]. Around the British Isles, Barnum's name may be synonymous with circuses, but his early passion was his American Museum, which opened on lower Broadway on 1st January 1842 and turned Barnum into one of the richest men in America. Barnum was fascinated with every aspect of 'entertainment', but the museum wasn't just about marvels of nature such as Caley and Tom Thumb; it promoted art, music, literature and crafts and as word-of-mouth grew it became the place to be, New York's most popular attraction, with 850,000 exhibits spread across four conjoined buildings. Waxworks, taxidermy and an aquarium added to the attractions, while a theatre provided a stage for performers, lecturers and Caley, Tom Thumb and their peers. Other areas must have come across as an early version of Tomorrow's World, with new technology ensuing crowds were dazzled by ivory carvers and glassblowers and panoramas from Niagara Falls to Peru.

It was into this world of wonders that Caley arrived, most likely

General Tom Thumb.

towards the end of the museum's heyday. The Circus World Museum in Baraboo, Wisconsin, first mentions Barnum with Goshen the year before Barnum's world came crashing down in 1865, the same year as the American Civil War ended. Having embarked on an ambitious project to create a new industrial heart for his adopted home of Bridgeport, Connecticut, Barnum's fortune was wiped out following a disastrous business deal. He disappeared off the entertainment radar, surfacing again in Europe with Tom Thumb, but returned to the States and by 1870 he was back on his feet. He regained control of many of his business interests, including the American Museum, and finally got to lead the industrial revolution of Bridgeport. At this time he was approached by circus managers W. C. Coup and his partner, Dan Costello, with a proposition – to create a huge travelling circus. Barnum set about recruiting his friends and performers, including Caley and Thumb, claiming it would eclipse any exhibition ever created anywhere in the world. The following year, on April 10th, 1871, P. T. Barnum's Grand

Phineas Barnum posing with one of his stars, Commodore Nutt.

Travelling Museum, Menagerie, Caravan and Circus opened in Brooklyn.

The circus in the US can be traced back to 1793, when an English equestrian rider, John Rickets, introduced a ring into his act and brought in acrobats, rope walkers and clowns. In the early 1800s, Hackaliah Bailey, a New York farmer, bought an elephant from his sea captain brother and the circus's love affair with elephants was born, although not everyone approved; Old Bet, as the elephant was known, was shot and killed by a thug in 1816, but that didn't stop Bailey preserving her remains and taking her on tour for another four years. Circuses floundered when Rickets' ship was wrecked on a journey back to England, with no one of his charisma to capture the public's imagination. Travelling menageries took their place, with entrepreneurs displaying wild animals and by the late 1830s they'd worked out how to combine the attractions of a menagerie with those of a circus – Isaac Van Amburgh dressed up as a Roman gladiator and stepped into a cage with

49

a lion, tiger, leopard and a panther, and in 1833 he became the first tamer to put his head into a lion's mouth. Van Amburgh had his critics; he was reported to beat the animals into submission with a crowbar, and was vilified for encouraging cruelty to animals.

When menageries introduced circus rings to present their equestrians and clowns, the line between menagerie and circus became blurred. Circuses travelled from town to town, slowly, as the wagons struggled with the weight and muddy country roads, and as the years passed they became increasingly complex affairs, with new types of acts added regularly, until by the 1850s there were approximately thirty circuses touring the US at any one time and they had established themselves as the major – and in many places, the only – form of entertainment. However, it was the work of Barnum, and his associates, that took the circus to another level.

At some point around the time that the Greatest Show was launched, a book was published by Barnum's American Museum. Entitled the *The History of Palestine and the Present Condition of Old Jerusalem, and the Life of Colonel Routh Goshan*, with a subheading *Biographical History and Adventures of Colonel Routh Goshan, the Arabian Giant*, it reproduced the fictitious stories that Caley told in his act and includes several illustrations of him in his role as a colonel in battle. At the end of the book it mentions 1870 being 'the present time', although the copy of the book Carlton obtained has the year 1880 below the publisher's details, marking it out as a reprint. While clearly a work of fiction, it does provide an insight into his act and does contain some elements of fact, from which Barnum and Caley, and the unnamed author, have spun the Giant's tale.

It opens with a look at giants as perceived by society, claiming they have been subject to a 'persistent and ungenerous tendency to underrate the merits of the elevated class', citing the fairytale of Jack the Giant-Killer as an example. Yet it talks about how each country has its own legends of giants and how they are known for their wartime exploits as much as they are for their size, claiming that both Samson and William Wallace were giants.

It's a curious read, spending many pages describing the races that he met and their histories and customs, not to mention several more on accounts from other famous travellers, which is clearly just padding to give the book a bit of weight. According to the story, Goshen was born in 1837 in Jerusalem, a city about which the author then spends several pages waxing lyrical, recounting some of its history and it is page thirteen of sixty before we pick up Goshen's story, with a claim that he was the youngest of fourteen children (close to the size of Caley's family – did they avoid thirteen as it was considered unlucky?), each of whom was a giant, as was their mother and father. Goshen was sent by his parents to Great Britain to benefit from a sound education and was entered into a military school in Dublin where he gained his early battlefield prowess.

If we are looking for further pieces of the Caley/Goshen jigsaw in the biography, they are there to be found. It mentions how Goshen mastered the English language, and accent, while in the British Isles, which would be convenient given Caley's background. It wouldn't take Einstein to question why an Arabian giant spoke perfect English, although he allegedly spoke another seven other languages for good measure.

From Ireland, he sailed to California aged eighteen, spending six months in Oregon, where the American Indians christened him 'Little Etalapass' (Little God) and he saved the lives of two natives by crushing a bear's head with a boulder that they couldn't even lift, which could be construed as a nod to some of the tales of Caley's antics as a young man. On hearing of the outbreak of the Crimean War, our man set out for Turkey, with a stop at the Sandwich Islands, and then onto South America and Mexico. When Goshen finally made it to Constantinople, his reputation and testimonials saw him awarded a rank of captain in one of the principal regiments of the Moslem army.

It's at this point that we are given a description of Goshen, and it's likely that this is one area where the author had to stick reasonably closely to the facts, as Caley would have been widely known and was still exhibiting.

The book says:

'No model ever used by a sculptor could be more accurate and

'The Life of Col. Goshan' published in 1880.

harmonious in outline than the body of this colossal yet amiable and charming gentleman. His vast expanse of chest gives token of herculean strength, while his dark, proud eyes and short upper lip give unmistakeable proof of the proud race from which he sprang. His hands and feet are remarkably small in proportion to his height and his hair is of the raven hue peculiar to the full-blooded Arabian. No one can converse with him for five minutes without experiencing the most kindly feeling toward him and the hosts of friends he daily adds to his list must be a source of great pleasure and satisfaction.'

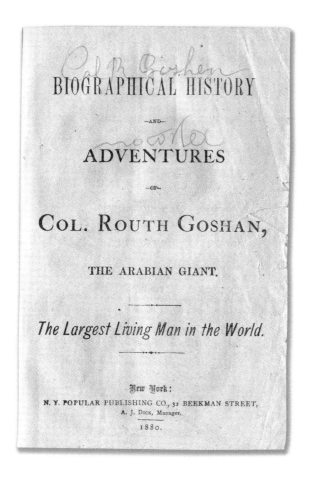

The title page has, scrawled across it in pencil, 'Col R Goshen no other'.
Sideshow people often signed and sold souvenirs whilst exhibiting and this most
probably is Caley's handwriting.

The story has Goshen critically injured in a charge against a Russian battery and succumbing to a fever, which left him bed-ridden for three months – another nod to the growing pains from his youth? – and he would have died, said the author, if it hadn't been for his amazing constitution. There follows a verse, where the speaker recalls his youth

An illustration from the book showing the Colonel in action.

and injuries in battle, but it's not clear if the author is attributing this verse to Goshen, or whether he has lifted it from elsewhere. If it is Goshen, the opening is yet another link between the two.

It opens:

> *My father was a farmer man*
> *With corn and beef in plenty,*
> *I mowed and hoed and held my plough*
> *And longed for one and twenty.*
> *My mind had quite a martial turn,*
> *I scorned the lowing cattle.*
> *I craved to wear a uniform*
> *And face the smoke of battle.*

It's at this point that things become a little confusing. On page fifty, the author has Goshen aged seventeen in 1854 and again leaving Europe for the United States, which contradicts the earlier claim that he had first left Ireland aged eighteen bound for California. In 1857 Goshen was back in Europe, visiting Holland and Austria, finding a wife along the way and fighting in the war between Austria and Italy. Returning to California, he then visited every republic in South America before sending for his wife to join him, only for her to fall victim to yellow fever.

After stays in China and Jerusalem, the author has Goshen returning to Mexico, fighting to repel the French, indeed leading two thousand men in resisting an attack of twelve thousand French. After several more skirmishes, Goshen was taken as a prisoner of war and sentenced to Martinique Island for the rest of his life, only to perform a daring escape and make his way to Texas and so on to New York, where he arrived in 1863, after which he began his stage career. This does, of course, fit in with the widely-held belief that Caley arrived in New York sometime in the early 1860s.

The book would account for many of the 'truths' printed about Caley, with the media and public unable – or unwilling – to see past the fictitious biography. Indeed, on the Circus Historical Society website[36], under the heading *Olympians of the Sawdust Circle: A biographical dictionary of the nineteenth century American circus*, is an entry on Goshen:

> Sideshow giant, known as 'The Palestine Giant'. Of Arabic parents, the youngest of 14 or 15 children, all remarkable for their size and strength. Served with distinction in the Crimean War and later in the Mexican army. P. T. Barnum is said to have met him on the street and hired him at once, showing him with the circus in the summer and exhibiting him in the NYC museum in the winter. It is said he received a salary of $40 a week and expenses. Was the largest giant Barnum produced, being advertised at 7' 6", shoulders 2' 6", and waist 77". Actual height measurement for his coffin was 7' 2". Height was accentuated by comparison with the dwarfs, Major Atom and Brig. Gen. Spec, who ran around his legs as he walked. In his prime, weighed 560 pounds.

The most interesting information from this reference is his wages, assuming this isn't more fiction – using 1875 as an average for Caley's career, the $40 then would equate to around $850 a week in today's money, depending on what conversion parameters you use.

Back in the real world, it's thought that Caley had married by this stage, although there is no mention in any research as to his wife's name. Information about Caley's affairs of the heart is rare; newspaper reports from the time of his death suggest he was married three times, but there is nothing to substantiate this. In a series of newspaper articles in 1935, Elsie Stryker, of Middlebush in Somerset County, New Jersey, said that in 1874 'the Goshens adopted Frances, a little six-year-old girl', after which the family travelled to England and Germany for a year, with Frances dancing before Queen Victoria. This is the only mention of such an event, although with Barnum having toured Europe with Tom Thumb and reportedly meeting Queen Victoria, perhaps this later report about Caley and Frances does have some basis in truth.

The American newspaper reports from this time that mention Caley reveal as much about Barnum as the Manx Giant. One story[37] tells of an argument between Goshen and another giant in Barnum's employ. Frenchman Jean Bihin was a good friend of Caley's, although they were both jealous of each other's exploits, not to mention the attention that was showered on their rival – and it was this petty jealously that saw the two of them threaten to kill the other after they traded insults, Goshen calling the Frenchman a 'Shanghai' and Bihin retorting with 'nigger'.

Having armed themselves with a club and a sword (it's not clear who had which), a crowd of museum workers appeared and tried in vain to separate the colossals. It wasn't long before the ensuing mayhem roused Barnum, who left his office to join the congregation.

'If you want to fight each other, maiming and perhaps killing one or both of you, that is your affair,' Barnum is reported to have said. 'But my interest lies here – you are both under engagement to me, and if this duel is to come off, I and the public have a right to participate. It must be duly advertised, and must take place on the stage of the lecture room. No performance of yours would be a greater attraction.'

Whether Barnum was being serious isn't clear – he may have been, given the charge he could have made on the door – but the proposition made Caley and Bihin see sense and they burst into laughter and shook hands.

Yet it wasn't just Barnum who was a canny operator. If there was a suggestion during his younger days that Caley may have been a touch slow, he seemed wise to the ways of the world as he grew older. He knew good publicity when he saw it and in 1871, coinciding with Barnum entering the circus business, Caley announced in the *Brooklyn Eagle*[38] that he would bet $5,000 to charity that he was the tallest man in the world. Today, with global communications what it is, that would be a challenge easily met. However, Caley must have guessed that the chance of anyone being able to edge him in the height stakes, at least amongst the *Eagle*'s readership, was slim at best. That said, he did claim to be eight feet tall and weigh in at 640lbs, which were slight exaggerations on his part, although it's unlikely anyone was going to argue with the man. It wouldn't be the last time Caley used the *Eagle* to his benefit, but in the meantime he was a regular fixture in adverts in the newspaper during the 1870s and by 1872 Caley was topping the bill of the human curiosities – there were, however, 'four living giraffes' above him – and witnessed by the 'elite of the metropolis, luxury and comfort combined in the most beautiful and brilliant amphitheatre in the world'.

By this time Caley's position within Barnum's circle had been cemented. The *Eagle*[39] has him heading the bill in an advert for the 'Second week of the Great Moral Museum, Menagerie and Hippodrome' and the Circus World Museum has references to him touring with Barnum, as the Arabian Giant, in 1873 and again in 1877, while the following year he was billed as the Palestine Giant.

In 1874, with his Greatest Show on Earth showing no sign of dipping in popularity, Barnum found a permanent home for his enterprise. The New York Hippodrome would later be known as Madison Square Garden and at the time was the largest public amusement structure ever built, housing in excess of 10,000 punters and costing a cool $150,000 to build.

The press notices and adverts from the time don't provide a great

Caley's adopted daughter, Frances.

amount of detail, but they do provide an insight into the workings of the shows. Barnum's Museum, Menagerie and Circus performed in a 'vast amphitheatre crowded with the elite of the metropolis'[40], complete with 'brilliant lights, enchanting music and luxurious seats'. The show opened daily from 11am till 10pm, with hippodrome performances at 2pm and 8pm, and general admission – including balcony seat in the circus – was fifty cents, children under ten in for twenty five cents. If you wanted a sofa seat on the parquette, it would set you back an extra twenty five cents, an extra fifty if you wanted cushioned armchairs.

There is a more expansive account in the *Brooklyn Eagle*[41] from 1879, which paints a colourful vision of the opening night of that year's

'Greatest Show' season, as well doing its bit to enhance Barnum's reputation:

> Barnum may well be counted among the benefactors of this race. He has done more to minister to the innocent enjoyment and hearty pleasure of the people of the United States for the past thirty odd years than any other one man in the country. Our fathers and mothers went to see Barnum's Museum, on the corner of Broadway and Ann Street, in the old days. They laughed at the woolly horse and the mermaid, but their hearts thrilled and the tears melted when Jenny Lind wooed them with her matchless song. And now their children take their youngsters to see 'the greatest show on earth' and the little ones dilate with wonder and pure delight, while the older heads confess that the sawdust ring, the dashing riders, the glitter and the spangles have not lost their old time charm.
>
> This immense exhibition may be said to be divided into two parts, the museum and the circus, and each is larger than any of its compeers. The museum contains the largest collection of animals outside the London Zoo, while the circus is far ahead of anything of the kind ever seen in this country or in Europe. This is not mere hyperbole, but is actual fact.

It continues:

> There are three immense tents, opening into each other, and the smallest of the three is as large as the usual circus tent. Entering the first, you find yourself in the wonders of the museum, which it would be utterly futile to attempt even to catalogue, but there are things that have never been seen before in this country. The first two tents are taken up with the museum and the menagerie. The latter includes ten elephants of all sizes, including two baby elephants, that make a tremendous crying and roaring when their comrades are away in the grand entrée. There is the black rhinoceros, the only one of his kind in the country. He lies in his cage snoring like a pig. There are two black elephants and they are a wonder, for they have never been shown before either in this country or in Europe… There are two polar bears, panting and

blowing, and wobbling about in the curious way peculiar to their kind. Then there are monkeys by the score and birds and beasts; two-footed, four-footed creeping things; in all, over three hundred animals are crowded under the two large tents.

Beyond is the crowning charm of the whole, the circus tent. This is 250 feet long by 140 feet wide and will seat comfortably 8,000 people...but the bell rings, the band dashes off in a grand march and every boy and man in the huge assembly is on the tiptoe of expectation, when the grand cavalcade enters, in all the pomp of purple, and gold, and crimson and scarlet, huge elephants, wry-necked camels, graceful giraffes and, oh, such horses! It is a long procession and each new feature is received with tremendous applause.

Finally, it disappears behind the curtain, and in come the "living curiosities, the tattooed Greek nobleman, Colonel Routh Goshen, the giant; Miss Minnie Keeler, the "Little Queen Mab" of the arena. Then comes Mr Carl Antony and his two royal stallions, Pasha and Marmeluke. Not a word does he say to them and they go through their evolutions guided only by his gestures. Then comes a wonderful balancing feat by William O'Hale Stevens. It is far ahead of anything the Japanese can show...

And on it goes; James Holloway, the 'boss' clown, the Egyptian jugglers, Miss Kate Stokes, a sensational bareback rider, acrobats the Herbert Brothers, *et al*, until the performance drew to a close at half past ten with John Batcheldor, with his 'great leaping feat when he turns and double somersaults over the back of six elephants'.

'Everything about the great exhibition is perfect and pure,' said the reviewer. 'It is no wonder that Barnum draws the cream of the country.'

Another advert[42] mentions the first appearance of the 'charming singers and dancers, the Goshen Sisters', but no other reference to them could be unearthed, so it's unclear whether Barnum was linking these women to Caley, possibly trying to pass them off as the Giant's sisters.

It's difficult, in this day and age, to appreciate just how big a name Barnum was and how popular the stars of his show were. But there was little else by way of entertainment and it's not too much of a stretch to imagine the likes of Tom Thumb, Commodore Nutt and Caley as the 'movie stars' of that era, with Barnum as Steven Spielberg and Peter Jackson rolled into one. Barnum and his stars were household names, with thousands flocking to see them every day and their personal lives made headline news, as Caley would one day discover.

Other newspaper adverts mention Caley with J. B. Johnson[43], the champion swimmer of the world, making his last appearance in America prior to his departure to Europe to contest an international swimming match with Paul Boynton, the hero of the straits of Dover. Elsewhere, an advert[44] for G. B. Bunnell's Dime Museum in Fulton Street, New York, claimed that three thousand visitors a day were passing through the turnstiles to see the likes of Caley, a family of German midgets – the smallest family in the world, of course – and the 'Leopard Boy, tattooed by nature'. Those three thousand, the advert said, proclaimed the museum as the 'best, largest, purest place of amusement worth ten times the price charged for admission'.

At Hooley's Opera House, the crowd flocked to see Miss Belle Howitt and her burlesque troupe in Jack the Giant Killer, with Goshen – again 'over eight feet tall' – as the eponymous giant.

Given this kind of coverage, it's clear that Caley appeared with other circuses and shows, suggesting that Barnum did not have exclusive rights to him. It's also evident that Caley had plenty of strings to his bow and wasn't just a sideshow attraction for people to come and stare at. Indeed, a 1930s cutting of the *Gouverneur Tribune Press*[45] had 'Colonel Goshen, the Arabian Giant' appearing in Van Amburg's Big Circus, with the claim of being the 'most stupendous, gigantic and colossal aggregation of freaks and curiosities ever assembled under canvas', Goshen appearing with 'Big Eliza, the fat girl, weighing nearly 500lbs; JoJo, the dog-face Russian boy and Zip, the missing link, half human and half ape'.

The flexibility of his arrangement with Barnum benefitted Caley, whom the *Brooklyn Eagle* said earned 'many shekels', and with his new-

A poster advertising an appearance by Col. Ruth Goshen alongside the world's smallest man, Commodore Nutt.

found wealth (indeed, perhaps because of it), Caley's heart was captured by a young woman called Augusta Mattice. It's difficult to place a time on his meeting with Mattice. The story is recounted in the *Brooklyn Eagle*[46] in 1879, but at the place where the article mentions the year they became acquainted, the printing is blurred; however, reading between the lines it appears Caley met her a couple of years before. However, it's entirely possible that he and Augusta met earlier and she was, in fact, Caley's wife when he adopted Frances.

Whatever the timing of their meeting, it took place in a Delancey Street boarding house on the east side of New York. Augusta Mattice was a 'tall and dark 25-year-old' who ran the boarding house in question. She claimed to be a widow (later disproved, the *Eagle* claimed) and an unsuspicious Caley spent a few months courting her before proposing. According to the *Eagle*, Caley and his bride then toured the States, Canada, Mexico, Europe and Palestine, but again some of these travels are likely to have been fabricated tales, most likely from Caley himself, although if Augusta was the woman he adopted Frances with, perhaps it would tie in with their reported tour of Europe and meeting Queen Victoria.

The Giant's happiness wasn't to last. Augusta left Caley for another man, J.W. Sweet, a story which was too good for the media to miss. The *Brooklyn Eagle* ran an article entitled 'Melancholy, the Matrimonial Experiences of colonel Routh Goshen'[47], which gave an extensive account of Caley's tale of woe. A subheading read 'The Greatest of Injured Husbands' and within the article Caley said it would 'not be well for the rascal' if he caught up with Sweet.

The article contains many items of fiction, particularly regarding his military past. It's a curious read, and a fascinating insight into journalism of that era. A further subheading, below the Matrimonial Experiences, read: 'The Turkish Giant, robbed of his wife, his educated goat, his money and his horse and carriage – the perfidy of a man whom he befriended – a very high life elopement which excites the show people – moving for a divorce'.

Assuming that some of the article is based in fact and not all exaggeration, it also paints a rare picture of what Caley was like as a person.

It goes on:

That matrimonial misery may afflict the highest as well as the lowest was never better illustrated than in the affliction which has

One of the many portraits of Caley as Colonel Ruth Goshen.

overtaken Colonel Ruth Goshen, the giant whose enormous figure has towered in Brooklyn for the past two weeks. The colonel is one of the most widely known celebrities of his class in the United States. His acquaintances agree that he possesses agreeable manners and a confiding disposition: and although in stature he might easily vie with the lofty inhabitants of Brobdignag[48], he is but a child in the dark and crooked ways of this wicked world.

Mrs Goshen had eloped with a showman and Caley – who readers would remember for 'his good-natured face, which beams from under his broad-rimmed hat, as big and shining as a locomotive headlight' –

was seeking a divorce.

The *Eagle* said he was of Hebrew and Turkish descent, gave Jerusalem as his place of birth, and said he was forty three, although he was actually mid-fifties by this time. It reported his height as seven feet eleven inches (in his stocking feet) and weight at 625lbs. With a ninety-five inch waist and ninety-one inches around the chest, this journalist well and truly had the measure of Caley.

> His arms are of the thickness of saplings and his fist possesses the ponderosity of the hammer of Thor. The Colonel has served in several eventful campaigns. He was in the Turkish army at Jerusalem and fought through the Crimean War, the war of Italian independence and the campaign of Maximilian in Mexico. His great height made him a fine target for the enemy; he was wounded in numerous engagements and at present has seventeen bullet homes in his body, which seem to have had as much effect as they would on the hide of the elephant or the rhinoceros.

It would appear that the journalist had read Goshen's fictional biography and such elaborations owed much to the showmanship of Barnum. His manipulative tall tales, not just for Caley, caught the public's imagination. Once recorded by newspapers, and indeed so-called biographies, the stories gained some element of respectability. Readers of the future will have understood that references to Norse mythology were journalistic fancies, and may have raised an eyebrow at the number of holes blasted in the Giant. But they would have had little reason to dispute the military campaigns attributed to Caley, and so the myths were perpetuated.

Best of all, though, is a first-hand account, which the *Eagle* claimed the Giant told a reporter in the Dime Museum at 430 Fulton Street. Under a subheading 'The Colonel's tale of woe', Caley told the journalist:

> She was a very pretty woman and before I found her out I thought a great deal of her. She was very well behaved toward me up to the time I discovered her infidelity. When she was true,

nothing was too good for her. She travelled with me almost all over the world. We went through the United States and three years ago, when I took Donald McKay and the Warm Spring Indians to Europe, she accompanied me.

We went through England, France, Germany, Russia, Italy and then I took her to my old home in Jerusalem. I always thought she was the finest woman in the world. We never had a cross word or a fuss of any kind at this time. I showered all sorts of gifts on her. Gold chains and necklaces and diamond rings were given as freely as water and she had all the money she wanted. Up to a year ago I had not the least reason to suspect her fidelity to me. At that time we were living on my farm at Clyde Station, New Jersey. An engagement was tendered me by the Harry Deacon Opera Company and I wanted her to accompany me on a tour through the provinces, but she said she was tired of travelling and refused to go with me. I thought it strange, but said nothing, and left her at home with our two adopted children, the servants and a man named J.W. Sweet, who I had rescued from poverty and given a home.

When I returned home from the West, I asked my wife for the key to my safe which had been entrusted to her care. She said the key had been left in New York for safe keeping, but I went to the place she designated and found her statement was false. On my return to Clyde Station, I found that my wife had run away with Sweet, taking with her about $10,000 in money and bonds which I had left in the safe. From the servants, I learned that Sweet had for months been living in improper relations with my wife.

This man Sweet was at one time the husband of Madame Sebastian, the circus rider, who was obliged by ill-treatment to leave him and get a divorce. My wife and he got away in time to save her life and that of her paramour. My first impulse was to follow them and kill them both, but the counsels of my neighbours and my own common sense made me think better of it, and leave their punishment to a higher authority than mine. Sweet and Mrs Goshen went to New York where they lived together until three weeks ago. All that Sweet cared for was money, for as soon as it was gone, he began a course of systematic abuse against my wife. Three weeks ago, he gave her a terrible beating and then ran away to Canada, where he is now in hiding. My wife is now reduced to the lowest depth of degradation, and has appealed to me for assistance, but I have sent word to her to go to Hades, and say that I sent her there.

The interview then entered the realms of the bizarre. Caley continued:

A few weeks ago, while I was away from home, Sweet and my wife went there and stole a horse and carriage and an educated goat, which I valued at $4,000. I thought everything of that goat. He could read, write and multiply. Sweet, I believe, has possession of him now. I have reason to believe that the robbery of my horse last December was a job put up by Sweet and my wife. It would not be well for the rascal if I could catch up with him.

The *Eagle* reporter told how Caley ended the interview with a mighty thump of his hickory cane that made the floor tremble. He seemed deeply affected when he told the writer that he expected a divorce at an early date. When he concluded his story, he arrayed himself in his blue scarlet uniform and his big helmet and mingled with the crowd which admired the dwarfs, the glass blowers, the St Denoit twins and the other wonders of the museum, of which all agreed that Colonel Routh Goshen was the greatest of all.

The following day, Caley was back in the *Eagle*[49] with a story under the headline 'The Greatest of Injured Husbands'. After likening the Giant to Gulliver discovering that no man is too big to be the subject of local prejudice, the article staunchly defended Caley, heaping plaudits on his character and reiterating the 'facts' from the previous day. However, it then attempted to determine the reasoning behind Mrs Goshen's disillusionment with her large-hearted man and it's here that it becomes clear the writer is having a bit of a joke, or at least we can only hope:

In the first place, we just realise that the presence of a man weighing 625 pounds, moving about in a small house, is apt to be attended with dangerous consequences. It is true that he would be useful in hanging pictures and sweeping cobwebs off the ceiling, but this advantage would be more than compensated for by the furniture he would thoughtlessly smash by sitting down suddenly in an ordinary chair, or the crockery he would upset by knocking his shins against the dinner table. A man of his size would be able to beat carpets pretty thoroughly, but how fearfully he would be in the way on wash days, and imagine the labour of cooking steaks and making coffee for such a person. Poaching eggs for the breakfast of a giant is work for a nimble-fingered giantess, and that Mrs Goshen is not. Beside, after a time the good old joke of asking a husband of nearly eight feet in height whether it is cold up there loses its point… Then again, the womanly instinct is to caress and call by endearing names the fortunate man of her choice. How can a woman caress a man eight feet high without standing on a chair to do it? How can she stroke his hair or pat his cheek without the assistance of a stepladder? These are all questions which Colonel Goshen ought to have asked himself before marrying and spending his money on dresses and gold chains.

Unfortunately for J. W. Sweet, the Giant did catch up with him, three years later in August 1882. A report in the *Quincy Daily Whig*[50] said Caley told a court that he met Sweet while walking along a boardwalk, only for Sweet to 'give him a malicious grin and use the most vulgar language in reference to Goshen's divorced wife and his mother', at which Caley drew a pistol and advised Sweet that he ought to shoot him, but would allow him to live in his degredation. Still, not wanting to let Sweet off completely, he hit him several times with his cane, inflicting head wounds. The court bound Caley over to the sum of $800 ahead of his hearing the following month, leaving the Giant free to rejoin the circus – but no account of the hearing has been found.

The discrepancies in the backgrounds contained within the *Brooklyn Eagle* and *Quincy* articles highlight how difficult it is to ascertain exactly what did happen between Caley and his wife. The Whig says Augusta and Sweet made off with $4,000 in silver, burned up $70,000 worth of bonds and took his goat, valued at $100, somewhat less than Caley's valuation in the *Eagle*.

Another quirky tale about the great Colonel Goshen appeared in the *New York Times*[51] in 1881, under a story called 'The Dwarfs and Giants: Who some of them are, and how they live'. It catalogues many of the characters exhibited by Barnum and others in the preceding two decades, and says of Goshen:

> There is Captain Goshen, the giant, and as big a specimen of humanity, perhaps, as the Middle States have ever produced. He was one of Barnum's company, and lived then, as he does now, in Newark. He entered a car one day coming up to the City. The car was in the condition half-filled cars will sometimes reach – with one man in each seat looking out of the window. The Giant looked slowly around the car, saw no whole seat vacant, and then going up to one of the single occupants of a seat said: 'If two of you little gentlemen will sit together we can all get along comfortably. If any of you sit with me, you'll get squeezed, that's all.' The gentlemen addressed changed his seat, and Goshen sat down, filling the entire seat, without two inches to spare on either side.

In this same year, Barnum, who at seventy-one was fourteen years older than Caley, teamed up with James Bailey, the young manager of the Cooper and Bailey Circus, and James L. Hutchinson. Their new creation was P. T. Barnum's Travelling World Fair, Great Roman Hippodrome and Greatest Show On Earth, which was later shortened to the Barnum and London Circus.

Caley was again part of the team, his time split between Barnum and other shows, including Nathan & Co's Circus in 1882, the same year as he was billed as the Knight of Palestine by Barnum. An anonymous newspaper cutting from 1883 told how the arrival in town of the Barnum, Bailey and Hutchinson Circus, as it was known at that time, was heralded by twenty-four marching elephants from the circus train at the railroad tracks to the circus grounds, a sight in itself worth the admission price. The circus also boasted 'two menageries, 30 cages of wild animals, a huge elevated stage for Olympic Game, a quarter-mile running track and, of course, three rings of circus performers'. Among its highlighted performers were 'three Zulu warriors, a tribe of Sioux Indians, Mexican vaqueros and cowboys from the plains, Australian cannibals and boomerang throwers, wild beast hunters in grotesque dress, 13 Nubians – and Goshen, the eight-foot giant'. Caley striding into town as part of this procession must have been a wondrous sight.

One of the other engagements Caley had in his diary at this time was at Brighton Beach, Brooklyn, a new resort created by William A. Engeman on several hundred acres of oceanfront property and named after the English south coast town. Visitors flocked to Brighton Beach in their thousands and the growing number of attractions was enhanced in 1883, when G. B. Bunnell opened a dime museum, showcasing[52] a 'convention of curiosities', including the Palestine Giant, Colonel Routh Goshen, who was outrageously billed as eleven feet tall, Major Tot, who weighed in at ten and a half pounds and the 'fat boy' Richard James, who measured 'nine feet around the waist'. Caley and his colleagues were in good company; that same year, Buffalo Bill Cody used Brighton Beach to stage a recreation of cowboy life, bringing with him a band of Sioux Indians and cowboys and cowgirls.

It's clear that Caley was still in demand as he approached his sixtieth birthday, but time eventually catches up with everyone. Caley lived to a much riper age than most giants, whose build often brings with it serious health problems. None of our references reveal Caley's state of health at any time in his life, other than the growing pains as a young man, but it's not a long stretch to imagine that by this time the life he'd led had started to take its toll.

Chapter 6

CURTAIN CALL

In 1874, Caley had bought a farm in Clyde, a town in Franklin Township within Somerset County, New Jersey. Today, Franklin has a population of just over 50,000 and has undergone major development over the last few decades, although it continues to retain some of its rural feel, with 19th century homes and tree-lined streets. Indeed, in 2008 Franklin was ranked fifth in *Money Magazine*'s list of 'America's Top 100 Best Places to Live'.

Originally, however, Franklin was a farming community and it has a fitting symmetry as the place where Caley spent his final years, given his childhood in Sulby. Clyde is in an area of the county known as Middlebush and Caley was soon known to locals as the Middlebush Giant. However, Caley found it difficult to hang up his plumed helmet for good, returning to touring in 1887, according to the Circus World Museum, and one final time with Barnum in 1889.

Caley's semi-retirement from the circus business did nothing to diminish his standing as the Middlebush Giant. In one of the articles discovered by Miss Edith Cowin, a New Jersey resident, the *New York Sun*[53] paints a vivid picture of Caley during his latter years as someone 'known for miles on every side of New Brunswick… not only for his conspicuous size and circus reputation, but [also for] his remarkable invention when applied to stories of his own adventures'. The *Sun* said:

> Certainly the people of the rural area of Clyde found plenty to talk and marvel over, as circus friends of Goshen arrived and departed in typical flamboyant manner. But eventually they became proud in their own way of this remarkable person in their midst. He

71

used to ride around the countryside, spinning yarns to the gaping crowds, driving a low, wide wagon, spanned by a single uncovered seat, drawn by two small mules and taking up most of the roadway. For these excursions the Colonel wore a scarlet plush jacket, which served to increase the effect of his already conspicuous size. His hat, a black sombrero, had a brim a foot wide.

Caley was proud of his achievements. He transformed one of the barns on his farm into a circus ring, filling it with artifacts from his career, although some curiosities he gave to neighbours, no doubt reinforcing his popularity in Middlebush. Caley must have been devastated then, when fire tore through his farm in the summer of 1888, destroying barns and stables and taking with it all his relics[54]. How much of an effect this had on the Giant can only be guessed at, but it might not be coincidence that his health started to fail around this time.

Looking back at Caley's life, recording it for future generations, there is a frustration that more information and records are not available. To have an insight into what was going through his mind when he left the Isle of Man, through England and on to Paris – most significantly his departure from France – would be fascinating. Even during his time in America, while there are many mentions of him in various reports, it's only really the *Brooklyn Eagle*'s accounts of his marital woe that come close to bringing Caley alive in the reader's mind.

There is a train of thought which suggests that, to measure a person's mark on the world, do not look at the news coverage generated by their life, but consider the reaction when that person dies. If this has merit, then it reflects highly on Caley.

On Tuesday, 12th February 1889, the Manx Giant passed away on his farm. Arthur Caley was sixty-four when he was laid to rest in Cedar Grove Cemetery in Franklin. Fearing grave robbers would target his final resting place, Caley asked to be buried in an unmarked location – and extra deep. Since then, a tombstone has been placed at the cemetery to commemorate him, but not at the exact location.

Several newspapers covered the Giant's death and his funeral.

According to a report in the *Fort Covington Sun*[55], a New York newspaper, Caley was a 'mulatto, born in this country, though he passed in the show bills for Belgian'.

The report read:

He was about 70, and was seven feet two inches, two feet six inches across the shoulders, 28 inches through the chest and his weight was 630 pounds. He was thrifty and accumulated quite a little property. The farmhouse of the dead giant was thronged with villagers long before the hour fixed for the funeral. The remains had been placed in a coffin eight feet long and three feet wide. It was covered with cloth and had been specially made for the deceased. After the funeral services were over, the coffin was borne on the shoulder of eight sturdy farmers to a wagon which was standing in the road about 100 yards from the house. Undertaker Van Duyn said he could not find a hearse large enough to hold the giant's coffin. The pall bearers had a hard struggle in carrying the remains down the incline leading from the house to the road and when they deposited the coffin in the wagon, beads of perspiration stood out on their foreheads. A large crowd followed the remains to the Middlebush Cemetery, where the internment took place. Colonel Goshen left an estate valued at about £10,000. He was married three times and divorced twice. He left his property to his married daughter, with whom he resided. One of his wives, who resided in Elgin, Illinois, will, it is said, contest the Giant's will.

Meanwhile, the *Franklin Township Library News*[56] suggested Caley was closer to seven five and 400 pounds, but agreed on the size of the coffin and the eight sturdy men, but claimed that they had such difficulty in removing Caley from the house, that the coffin was left on the front porch while his body was removed on a carpet sling via an upstairs window.

Under the headline 'The Giant is Dead', the *New York Times*[57] claimed Barnum's Giant had been ill for months from a complication of diseases, culminating in dropsy, from which he died. The obituary read:

Colonel Goshen was literally one of the biggest guns in the show business. Everybody who went to Barnum's Circus in past

THE GIANT IS DEAD.

THE FAMOUS COL. GOSHEN EXPIRES AT HIS NEW-JERSEY HOME.

NEW-BRUNSWICK, N. J., Feb. 13.—Col. Ruth Goshen, Barnum's big giant, died at his home at Clide, near Middlebush, yesterday afternoon. He had been ill for months of a complication of diseases, which culminated at length is dropsy, and it was from that disease that he died.

Col. Goshen was literally one of the biggest guns in the show business. Everybody who went to Barnum's circus in past years remembers him. He was a Prussian by birth and a Colonel by reputation. He differed from most giants in that he was physically almost perfectly formed. He was compactly built, with muscles solid as iron, and not a spare inch of flesh on his body. His great weight, therefore, was due to his size alone, and not to a superabundance of flesh. The Colonel was seven feet in height, though the bill boards set him down at eight, and indeed he was that when he put on his helmet and donned his high-heeled boots. He was well educated, master of many languages, including French, German, English, and Spanish, and was a man of fine presence and address. He weighed 575 pounds.

The Colonel was nearly 70 years of age. He had been married three times and divorced twice. He left a daughter, an extremely pretty girl, who was recently married. His last days have been spent upon his Clyde farm, which he purchased on his retirement from circus life. His home was a great curiosty to his country neighbors. One of the barns had been fitted up as a circus ring, and was filled with curiosities collected in his travels and arranged with considerable taste. Many of these curiosities were destroyed recently by fire and some of the others he distributed among his neighbors.

The account of Caley's death in the New York Times.

years remembered him. He was a Prussian by birth and a colonel by reputation. He differed from most giants in that he was physically almost perfectly formed. He was compactly built, with muscles solid as iron, and not a spare inch of flesh on his body. His great weight, therefore, was due to his size alone and not to a superabundance of flesh. The Colonel was seven feet in height, though he bill boards set him down at eight, and indeed he was that when he put on his helmet and donned his high-heeled boots. He was well educated, master of many languages, including French, German, English and Spanish, and was a man of fine presence and address. He weighed 375 pounds.

Much of the *New York Times* account seems to be rooted in the fabricated Goshen biography published by Barnum, and there are wild variations in height and weight in the different reports. What was Caley's true height and weight in his later years? Having retired from active circus life, it's possible his weight could have gone either way, although perhaps some weight loss, given his illnesses and general wear and tear on his body, is more likely, and certainly it's not unheard of for a person to lose a few inches in height as they age.

The *Fort Covington* and *New York Times* reports both suggest Caley was married three times, but again this may have been exaggeration, either from Caley in life or the media in his death. It's difficult to know. A claim of multiple wives is at odds with the knowledge passed down by his family, but yet again there is no name given – was this 'third wife' still Augusta Mattice, continuing to harass Caley even in death?

Perhaps the most important of these reports, when looking at the overall mystery of Caley and Goshen – and considering any doubts that the two men were one in the same – appeared in the *New York Times*[58] under the heading Contesting Colonel Goshen's will:

New Brunswick, New Jersey – It is reported that before his death Colonel Routh Goshen, the biggest giant Barnum ever exhibited, made a statement, giving his true name and the place of his birth. He said that his name was Arthur Crowley and that he was born in the Isle of Man about 70 years ago. Goshen's will is being contested by his third wife, who lives in Elgin, Illinois, and from whom he was not divorced.

Clearly, Crowley isn't Caley, but in such circumstances it's understandable if a name was misheard, misquoted or, more likely, written down incorrectly by someone so unfamiliar with such surnames.

Ruth Serjeant's research saw her contact the New York Public Library for details on Goshen, but she was frustrated to find it held just one photograph, undated, with the figure pictured identified as 'Barnum's Giant'. However, Serjeant had struck lucky in the form of Edith Cowin who had visited the Island shortly before Serjeant began her investigation into Caley.

Miss Cowin found articles in the *New York Sun* in 1889 reporting Caley's death, one of which was the source of the story that appeared in the *Manx Sun* later that year, and these led her to Middlesex County in New Brunswick to find a copy of Goshen's will.

She told Serjeant: 'A gentleman in the surrogate's office referred me across the street to the law office of a 92-year-old lawyer who knew Goshen personally. I visited the old gentleman, who told me that he knew him well as a boy… [and] that his father was the lawyer who handled Colonel Goshen's estate. He could remember no details about him except that he told me of a terrible time the undertaker had in getting the body out of the house.'

Miss Cowin visited Somerset County and obtained a copy of the will and death certificate, which she sent to Serjeant, before moving on to Middlebush, where she met the daughter of Goshen's adopted daughter, Frances.

'This lady is very feeble and about 75-years-old,' continued Miss Cowin. 'She told me that her mother died in New Brunswick on 12th November 1949… [and] had travelled all over the world with Colonel Goshen from the time she was about fifteen.' Frances' daughter showed Miss Cowin a 'pamphlet' about Goshen, which appears to have been a copy of the fictional biography about his military exploits. The age on the death certificate, according to Serjeant, was the same as Caley's, while all other questions were answered with 'not known'. The will, with a codicil, was dated 28th January 1889 and named three beneficiaries – the first was Frances and the second a friend of the Giant's, and a dispute between these two meant that, according to Serjeant, by the time the situation had been resolved in 1893, the Giant's estate 'had been sold, his debts paid, and nothing was left for the beneficiaries'.

What really piqued Serjeant's interest was the name of the third beneficiary; Margaret Gelling. 'What name could be more Manx!' wrote Serjeant. 'Why should such a name, if not proof of Goshen's origins, appear in the will of this Palestine Giant?'

In the list of marriages in Lezayre, Serjeant found reference to a Margaret Caley marrying Robert Gelling on 26th December 1835. As no parentage was included in the records, there was nothing to confirm to Serjeant that this Margaret Caley was Arthur's sister. However, Serjeant's accomplice, Miss Cowin, again came up trumps.

'I spent this afternoon [6th August 1962] at the Newspaper Directory Division of the New York Public Library,' she told Serjeant, 'and am delighted to report that I traced a Margaret Gelling, in the *City Directory of Rochester, New York*, as follows: 1885, Margaret Gelling, widow of Robert Gelling, [up to the final entry in] 1909, Margaret C Gelling died 23rd December 1909, aged 94.'

The ages matched, but further evidence sealed it. The death certificate and obituaries confirmed the connection, with the most comprehensive report in the *Democrat and Chronicle*[59]. It read: '… Margaret Gelling, in her 95th year. She leaves three daughters… Mrs Gelling was born in the Isle of Man.'

The death certificate revealed her father to be Arthur Caley and her mother Ann Cullier – Kewley, another Manx surname confusing the person taking down the details – with Margaret's place of birth as 'England', which Serjeant notes was often used in American records to

The most commonly used photograph of Caley. But who is pictured with him - his wife, sister or daughter?

signify any part of the British Isles. Serjeant was, therefore, satisfied that the Caley/Goshen enigma had been solved. Yet she arrived at this conclusion without knowing one major piece in the puzzle.

Either Arthur Caley or his sister Margaret sent a large photograph from America of Routh Goshen to Caley's family, who still lived in the house next to the Sulby Glen Hotel. The picture remained hanging in the hall of that house until 2005, when it was removed to another location by the family.

As can be seen from the photograph (opposite), it has suffered from loss of background detail due to the effects of hanging in the hall for more than a century, where sunlight may have taken its toll. The giant figure in the picture was recognised by the family as their own Arthur Caley, which is surely evidence enough to end any doubt. However, doubt does exist regarding the identity of the woman in the picture. The photograph is the most commonly-used of Caley and the woman in question is always described as his wife. However, in recent years it has been suggested that the woman could either be his sister Margaret, or Frances, although the photograph would have had to have been taken late in Caley's life for this to be his daughter, who was born in 1868.

Latterly, more information – to which Serjeant would not have been privy – came to light. In 1980 Vivien Teare, Juliene's mother, contacted an Elsie Stryker through the Middlebush Reformed Church to inform her that the Middlebush Giant was, in fact, Arthur Caley of Sulby. Miss Stryker had written a *History of Middlebush* in 1935, which was published as a series of articles for a local newspaper and subsequently published in 1963 as a book, entitled *Where The Trees Grow Tall*.

Interestingly, Elsie's letter mentions a challenge by the *Guinness Book of World Records* to Caley's height and weight and includes reference to the Giant's baptism just days before he died:

> Dear Mrs Teare
>
> Our minister, the Rev Ronald Vanderbeek, has asked me to answer your letter of May 16th which he received a few days ago concerning the Sulby Giant. We are greatly interested in this unusual man, whom we know as the Middlebush Giant.
>
> As I note some of the facts we have recorded or heard, you will see a few discrepancies between your account and our's, the most serious being the year of his birth. Your date is 1824; our's 1837. I regret this difference and so not know how to explain it. We would like everything we have to be correct and would appreciate your comments and corrections.

In 1935 I was asked to write a history of Middlebush, a small village in Somerset County, New Jersey. It appeared in a series of articles in a small local newspaper. Later, in 1963, this history was printed by the Franklin Township Historical Society as part one of a book entitled Where the Trees Grow Tall. A second printing was necessary in 1977.

In a chapter entitled People and Places to Remember, there is, of course, a section about the Middlebush Giant, Colonel Ruth Goshen. I wrote: 'He is believed to have been the world's largest man. He measured 28 inches across the chest, two feet six inches across the shoulders, and had a 77-inch waistline. He was 7 feet 11 inches tall and weighed 620 pounds. Some sources say he was born in Jerusalem May 5, 1837. He travelled extensively in his early years.'

Just a few hours ago I learned that the Guinness Book of World Records has challenged our figures regarding his height and weight, saying that he was seven feet five and a half inches tall and weighed considerably less than 620 pounds, perhaps a little more than 420.

The statement 'some sources say he was born in Jerusalem', has not been taken seriously, but has been regarded as propaganda to add glamour to his connection with the Barnum and Bailey Circus, with which he travelled for some time. We would appreciate knowing the truth about his family, for we have heard that he was the youngest of a family of 14 children, all of whom were remarkable for size and strength.

Colonel Goshen's gravestone was erected by the Cedar Grove Cemetery Association in about 1972. It was understood that he had stated in his will that he wished his place of burial to be unmarked. However, since almost a hundred years had elapsed since his death, the cemetery association felt that they were justified in violating his request because of the community's pride in having had such a famous man in its midst. It would also prove that his existence was not a mere myth, as some people seemed to believe.

In our Middlebush Reformed Church records we find that

Colonel Ruth Goshen was received into membership on confession of his faith – a sick-bed conversion, December 16, 1888. He was baptized February 12, 1889. His home was a mile away from our Church.

In 1874, the Goshens adopted Frances, a little six-year-old girl. Shortly after that she travelled a year with them in England and Germany, along with a family of Indians. Little Frances danced before Queen Victoria of Great Britain. Years later she married Henry Sylvester. Their home was in the village of Middlebush. Her gravestone, near the Giant's, and bears the inscription Frances C Sylvester 1968-1949. I assume that the initial C is for Caley.

The following paragraph from the book *Where the Trees Grow Tall* may be of interest to you:

'Mrs Bertha Totten (a resident of Middlebush) relates that her husband, the late Arthur B Totten, was one of the pallbearers at the Giant's funeral. The great problem was what to do about the eight foot four inch coffin. It could not be gotten into the house. The solution was to leave it on the front porch, cut the window much larger, and bring the body out on a carpet sling.'

The above mentioned book also contains a picture of the giant and one of his very pretty little adopted daughter. If you are interested in obtaining a copy or copies of this book I shall be glad to send you as many as you would like. It sells for $7.50 per copy.

I sincerely hope that you will receive this letter in time for your celebration. I send my greetings to your church at this important time and pray that it may be blessed, in its ministry in the village of Sulby for many years to come.

If you ever visit America again, please come and visit us. You will receive a warm welcome.

Sincerely

Miss Elsie B Stryker

So Caley was Goshen; Goshen was Caley. The Giant had reinvented himself in the US after the mysterious events of Paris and lived a full and eventful life, based largely around P. T. Barnum and his various entertainments.

Caley's grave in Middlebush Cemetery. For many years his grave was unmarked, at his request, and this stone is more of a memorial than marking the exact location of his final resting place.

And what of Barnum? When Caley retired to his farm, the showman continued his attempts to bewitch and bedazzle the public with even more extravagant shows. By 1888, he and Bailey had created the Barnum and Bailey Greatest Show on Earth, which then became the Barnum and Bailey Circus and toured the world. Barnum was, it's claimed, the first circus owner to move his shows by train, although some historians suggest Bailey was the brains behind this move. Regardless of who took the plaudits, Barnum's love affair with the railway was short-lived; he died at home in his sleep on 7th April 1891, two years after Caley, and was buried in Mountain Grove Cemetery, Bridgeport, which, quite fittingly, he'd designed. Ever the businessman, it's said his final breath was used to enquire what the takings had been that day at Madison Square Garden.

But there are two final mysteries to reveal in the Caley story, the second of which may well be pure coincidence. According to Caley's obituary in the *Plattsburg Sentinel*[60], the United Reformed Church Minister who performed the funeral also took a deathbed confession. The paper claimed the Giant had confessed to committing 'a dark crime early in his career'. Was Caley confessing to his involvement in the insurance scam in Paris?

According to the *Sentinel*, the Giant told the minister he'd always wanted 'to die with his boots on', but when questioned about Caley's confession, the Minister kept his own counsel.

However, this claim was in turn disputed by the *New York Times* report, which claimed: 'The statement that the giant made a confession to his pastor that implicated the Colonel in a serious crime, is denied by the Minister. He says that Goshen merely confessed that all the stories told of him by himself were lies or exaggerations, and professed penitence for minor backslidings.'

The twist in the tail is that the Minister who took Caley's confession was, according to Miss Stryker, a Dr James Levevre – a surname that bears an uncanny similarity to that of the man who wrote to Ann Caley informing her of Arthur's death in Paris some thirty-six years earlier.

What's more, the spelling of the Minister's name is not consistent; The *Fort Covington Sun* calls him the Reverend Le Ferre, the *New York Times* names him as the Reverend J. L. Le Fevre, while Ruth Serjeant calls him James Lefevre, which is the same spelling as that of Etienne in Paris.

So – Levevre, Le Ferre, Le Fevre and Lefevre – surely this is no more than a remarkable coincidence? Because, if it's not, it points to Caley and Etienne being in league and covering up a decades-spanning deception. It's another curious possibility that Caley took to his grave and for which we will most likely never be able to determine a definitive answer. An unlikely coincidence? Maybe. But given the events that took place in Paris, perhaps not beyond the realms of possibility.

Whatever the truth, the Manx Giant was finally dead, thirty-six years after his first 'death'. He'd enjoyed a relatively long life, for a giant, and come a long way from his humble beginnings as a farmer in Sulby, rubbing shoulders with many of the stars of his era. But more than that, he'd been part of their circle, and remained a popular figure with the public throughout, be it as a sideshow attraction in a museum, a part of the Greatest Show on Earth or as a neighbour to the residents of Middlebush.

Caley will be remembered as one of the most colourful characters in Manx history, partly because of his exploits, but also because of the mystery that surrounds his life. He was, most likely, the tallest Manxman who ever walked this fair Isle, or at least that we have on record. The chances are, it will be a long time before the Island sees his like again, if indeed it ever does.

ENDNOTES

1 Giants: The Vanished Race of Mighty Men, Roy Norvill, published 1979
2 Website *The Brews of the Guilcaugh, Andreas*
3 Rural Architecture in the North of the Isle of Man, Sue Cannell, published 2001
4 Cast a Giant Shadow, John Kleiman, published 2001
5 Manx Sun – 20th September 1848
6 Isle of Man Daily Times, 15th October 1947
7 *Andreas*, Sally McCambridge, (funded by Manx Heritage Foundation), 2005
8 Shining by the Sea, Constance Radcliffe, Manx Heritage Foundation, 1989
9 Ramsey Courier, 13th June 1958
10 Isle of Man Family History Society Journal, Vol 12 No 1, February 1990. Letter was originally published in Mona's Herald 1852. Complete text of letter 'News from the Gold Diggings' can be seen at:
   http://www.isle-of-man.com/manxnotebook/famhist/v12n1.htm#5-6
   the Family History Society journals reproduced by Frances Coakley in her 'Manx Compendium'
11 *Manx Sun*, March 12th 1853
12 *Manx Sun* – 3rd May 1851
13 *Gorry, Son of Orry*, Clucas Joughin, published 1903 by Jarrolds
14 *Manchester Guardian*, 2nd July 1851
15 *Manchester Guardian*, 5th July 1851
16 *Manchester Guardian*, 12th July 1851
17 *Manchester Guardian*, 16th July 1851
18 *Manchester Guardian*, 30th August and 3rd September 1851
19 *Manchester Guardian*, 13th September 1851
20 *La Presse*, 25th January 1852
21 *La Presse*, 2nd February 1852
22 *La Presse*, 23rd February 1852
23 *A la memoire du colosse de Rhodes. Le Geant Ecossaise, Sir Arthur Caley*, Adolphe Joly, published in 1852
24 Nouvelle Heloise – Epistolary Novel by Jean-Jacques Rousseau, philosopher of the enlightenment whose political ideas influenced the French Revolution, was quite sexist and who didn't believe in educating women
25 *La Presse*, 24th December, 1852
26 *La Presse*, 7th January 1853
27 *Manx Worthies; or, Biographies of notable Manx men and women*, Arthur William Moore, published 1901

28 *Brooklyn Eagle*, 8th January 1879
29 *It's a Fact*, 'Dusty' Miller, published in the Isle of Man Examiner
30 *The Mystery of Arthur Caley*, Ruth Serjeant, the Manx Giant Journal of Manx Museum, vol. VI, no79, p. 172-176, 1962-1963
31 *Manx Sun*, 9th March 1889
32 *Colours of Enhancement: Theater, Dance, Music, and the Visual Arts of the Middle East*, edited by Sherifa Zuhur, Published by The American University in Cairo Press, 2001
33 *Manx Millennium*, *Isle of Man Examiner* supplement, published August/September 1999
34 www.pattkelley.com
35 Barnum Museum, 820 Main Street, Bridgeport, CT 06604. www.barnum-museum.org
36 www.circushistory.org/Olympians/OlympiansG.htm
37 www.electricscotland.com/history/barnum/chap10.htm
38 *Brooklyn Eagle*, 28th February 1871
39 *Brooklyn Eagle*, 25th November 1872
40 *Brooklyn Eagle*, 23rd November 1872
41 *Brooklyn Eagle*, 29th April 1879
42 *Brooklyn Eagle*, 12th May 1875
43 *Brooklyn Eagle*, 8th May 1875
44 *Brooklyn Eagle*, 13th January 1879
45 *Gouverneur Tribune Press*, 25th March 1936
46 *Brooklyn Eagle*, 8th January 1879
47 *Brooklyn Eagle*, 8th January 1879
48 The land of Giants in *Gulliver's Travels*
49 *Brooklyn Eagle*, 9th January 1879
50 *Quincy Daily Whig*, 17th August 1882
51 *New York Times*, 23rd October 1881
52 www.brooklynpubliclibrary.org
53 *New York Sun*, 3rd March 1889
54 *New York Times*, 10th July 1888
55 *Fort Covington Sun*, 7th March 1889
56 *Franklin Township Library News*, Spring Newsletter 2005
57 *New York Times*, 14th February 1889
58 *New York Times*, 11th March 1889
59 *Democrat and Chronicle*, 24th December 1909
60 *Plattsburg Sentinel*, 22nd February 1889

INDEX